Praise for Corrupt Communication

MYTHS THAT TARGET CHURCH LEADERS

I am very encouraged by *Corrupt Communication: Myths That Target Church Leaders* written by Bill and Laura Bagents. Having served as a shepherd for five years, this book would have been very valuable for me at that time. I want to encourage all elders, Bible school teachers, ministers, and deacons to take the time to read this book. It would be very beneficial for parents as well.

— MONTE TATOM, (EDD, AUBURN UNIVERSITY) WORKS IN CHRISTIAN HIGHER EDUCATION AND HAS SERVED AS A SHEPHERD AT CREEKWOOD CHURCH OF CHRIST IN MOBILE, ALABAMA.

Corrupt Communication: Myths That Target Church Leaders is a must read for every eldership in the great brotherhood of Christ. Bill and Laura Bagents have done us great service in providing this manual for us. How thoughtful and insightful it is. Because communication is so important, everyone should read it though it is targeted to leaders. *Corrupt Communication* needs wide circulation for improved relationships and happy work in the Kingdom.

— ANDY KIZER, MINISTER FOR THE
SALEM CHURCH OF CHRIST, FLORENCE,
ALABAMA

In their new book, *Corrupt Communication: Myths That Target Church Leaders*, the Bagentses have written as always in very succinct language. Their little book is remarkably adept at offering practical, everyday applications of scriptural truth in very simple, brief, concise, and cogent sentences. It can very easily be a quick read, but it would be wise, and far more profitable for the reader to slow down and allow to soak what they have said. Bill will often in his classes speak of things being profitable "on multiple levels." He urges, "Speak the truth in love," and urges "not with flattery or manipulation, but faithful optimism." As always the Bagentses are at their best in this new book with clear, logical, and convincing simple sentences. It is a rich and profitable read.

— JERRY SELF, MEMBER OF THE
HERITAGE CHRISTIAN UNIVERSITY
BOARD OF DIRECTORS

Communication is the glue that holds all relationships together. Good communication is vital to the success of all personal and business relationships as well. Bill and Laura do a masterful job of breaking down many common communication barriers that seem to plague multiple relationships across the board. Wisdom and key communication strategies can be found in this book for those in any leadership position, especially for those who hold a leadership role in the church. Bill and Laura's experience as a Christian couple and the heart of a seasoned elder and his wife shine through in the pages of this book.

— RALPH RICHARDSON, MINISTER,
NEW HOPE CHURCH OF CHRIST,
READYVILLE, TENNESSEE

CORRUPT COMMUNICATION

Myths That Target Church Leaders

🔥 🔥 🔥

BILL BAGENTS
LAURA S. BAGENTS

HERITAGE
CHRISTIAN UNIVERSITY
PRESS

Corrupt Communication: Myths That Target Church Leaders

Copyright © 2022 by Bill Bagents and Laura S. Bagents

Published by Heritage Christian University Press

Manufactured in the United States of America

Cataloging-in-Publication Data

Bagents, Bill (William Ronald), 1956-

Corrupt communication: myths that target church leaders / Bill Bagents and Laura S. Bagents

Heritage Christian Leadership Institute Series

p. cm.

ISBN 978-1-7374751-4-9 (paperback) 978-1-7374751-5-6 (ebook)

Library of Congress Control Number: 2021923940

1. Communication. 2. Christian leadership. I. Author. II. Bagents, Laura Lynn Stegall, 1960-. III. Title. IV. Series.

253—dc20

Cover design by Brad McKinnon and Brittany Vander Maas.

Scripture quotations are from the ESV® Bible (The Holy Bible, English Standard Version®), copyright © 2001 by Crossway, a publishing ministry of Good News Publishers. Used by permission.

*To the excellent church leaders God has allowed us to know—
people of substance, integrity, kindness, and wisdom—who have
watched for our souls and blessed our lives. We couldn't be who
we are without you.*

Acknowledgements

We express our thanks to the Heritage Christian Leadership Institute for allowing us to write under their banner. We are thankful to Andy Kizer for improving the book with his suggestions. We are grateful to Jamie Cox, Brad McKinnon, and the team at Heritage Christian University Press for major patience and painstaking editorial effort. Thanks to Brittany Vander Maas for assisting Brad with the cover.

We owe much to those who keep teaching us about communication, particularly within church settings. Our partnership with God's church and her leaders continues to be blessed. Some negative examples are shared; we don't mean them as insults or assertions of superiority. We mean them as warnings and words to the wise because we owe it to God to improve.

A word from Bill: Even for "my" books that haven't listed Laura as co-author, she was. It's not just the excellent proofreading skill; it's reading for heart, substance, and improved expression. Anything I do, she helps me do better.

Heritage Christian Leadership Institute

The Mission of the Heritage Christian Leadership Institute is to provide workshops, seminars, and resources that train godly servant-leaders who can serve as leaders in congregations, families, and communities with an emphasis on training elders and deacons.

A Heritage Christian Leadership Institute resource in cooperation with Heritage Christian University Press

Bible Abbreviations

Old Testament

Gen	Genesis
Exod	Exodus
Lev	Leviticus
Num	Numbers
Deut	Deuteronomy
Josh	Joshua
Judg	Judges
Ruth	Ruth
1–2 Sam	1–2 Samuel
1–2 Kgs	1–2 Kings
1–2 Chr	1–2 Chronicles
Ezra	Ezra
Neh	Nehemiah
Esth	Esther
Job	Job
Ps	Psalms
Prov	Proverbs
Eccl	Ecclesiastes

Song	Song of Solomon
Isa	Isaiah
Jer	Jeremiah
Lam	Lamentations
Ezek	Ezekiel
Dan	Daniel
Hos	Hosea
Joel	Joel
Amos	Amos
Obad	Obadiah
Jonah	Jonah
Mic	Micah
Nah	Nahum
Hab	Habakkuk
Zeph	Zephaniah
Hag	Haggai
Zech	Zechariah
Mal	Malachi

New Testament

Matt	Matthew
Mark	Mark
Luke	Luke
John	John
Acts	Acts
Rom	Romans
1–2 Cor	1–2 Corinthians
Gal	Galatians
Eph	Ephesians
Phil	Philippians
Col	Colossians
1–2 Thess	1–2 Thessalonians

Contents

CORRUPT
COMMUNICATION

Introduction

"Let no corrupting talk come out of your mouths, but what is good for building up ..." (Eph 4:29). What Paul wrote to and for every Christian is extra true for church leaders. We love the wisdom, balance, and depth of Scripture. Immediately after James wrote, "Not many of you should become teachers, my brethren ...," he added a major discussion of the dangers and difficulties of careful, controlled, consistent speech (Jas 3). He provided one of the Bible's clearest contrasts of corrupt versus godly communication. And he directed it primarily to leaders.

Satan has been a corruptor of communication from the earliest pages of Scripture. We all know the famous "not" in the devil's tale (Gen 3:1–5). The devil is efficient; he's "original" only when he needs to be. Otherwise, he doesn't reinvent the wheel. Lies worked with Eve in Genesis 3, and he's been ruining communication ever since. He's even willing to learn from God; that's Babel in Genesis 11. (But that's Satan. He has absolutely nothing "original." All he can do is corrupt what God has made.) This lesson from Genesis 11 stands clear: If you want plans thwarted and people scattered, stop their communication. It's amazing how quickly plans fall apart.

Moving to the New Testament, those who wanted Jesus killed hid their motives and hired liars (Matt 26:59–68). They twisted His words and took them out of context. They practiced both selective hearing and selective memory. They trusted their assumptions and their flawed leaders more than they trusted God's word (John 18:12–14, Matt 27:15–26). And we know the horrendous results of this corrupt communication conspiracy. Paul faced a similar attack in Acts 21:27–30.

The devil isn't above blunt tactics and misuses of Scripture (Matt 4:1–11). He will use the easy road when that works, but obvious temptations are often just his initial attempts. It's like the guy on the mound giving you a high pitch to elevate your eyes before offering the low curve. Satan's best temptations are subtle and nuanced. They're wrapped in smoke, mirrors, fog, frustration, and fatigue. The packaging may be ever new, but the tools and techniques are as old as Eden. This is a book about the devil's better efforts, particularly those that target church leaders' communication.

Disclaimers and Recommendations

We'd never promise that every myth promoted by the devil will come exactly as we phrase it. Satan is skilled at tailoring his deceits to the person and the situation at hand. Read the cons expansively. Don't let a bit of window dressing hide the hook.

We'll never be wise or observant enough to create an exhaustive list of the devil's deceptions. Read the ones we list suggestively and creatively. "How might the tempter tweak this one to attack me and mine?" "What variations of this lie have I already faced?"

Please resist the temptation to say of any myth, "This could never happen to me! I'd never believe this." An extra-biblical proverb warns, "Don't dare the devil." It's excellent counsel. Who'd have foreseen Abraham surrendering to fear and lying about his wife twice (Gen 12:10–20 & 20:1–18), Joshua forgetting to pray (Josh 9:14), or Barnabas becoming a source of discouragement (Gal 2:11–13)? Proverbs 16:26, Matthew 6:13, and 1 Corinthians 10:12 offer major reminders. It would bless you to read this book with your Bible in hand. Even the strongest church leaders never become "unconnable." (Sorry, but we will coin a word from time to time.) The most dangerous cons are those that quietly lead us in comfortable and preferred directions. They're the ones that we don't even notice.

Please don't make too much of the order of the temptations within this book. While we attempted some clumping of related myths, much of the order is subjective. While a bit of repetition is unavoidable, we tried to write each contemplation as its own stand-alone unit.

Myth 1

COMMUNICATION IS OVER-RATED.

S atan should face an uphill battle with this dangerous myth. God chooses to reveal Himself through both creation and Scripture (Ps 19, Rom 1:18–21). Our ability and desire to communicate are two of the ways that we are made in God's image (Gen 1:26–27). The biblical emphasis on listening is well known (Prov 1:1–9 & 18:13, Luke 9:35, Jas 1:19–20). And common sense stands with the biblical record. Virtually everything we do with others both flows from and relies on accurate communication.

What gives communication a bad name with some church leaders? Well-meaning brethren sometimes become so enamored with the importance and the literature of communication that they overemphasize. They promote the latest theory as if it's THE ANSWER to major, longstanding needs. Sometimes experts overstate statistics when motivating people to improve their communication skills. For example: "80% of marriage problems flow from poor communication" or "70% of church conflicts are caused by communication errors." While those numbers may be accurate, some inaccurately hear them to claim, "All people need to do in order to solve and prevent problems is to talk to one another." Sometimes, church leaders have been burned during earnest attempts to communicate, and their scars remind them of the dangers. And, of course, evil and error constantly misuse communication strategies.

There's the odd statement, "90% of communication is nonverbal." (The exact number will vary, but 90 is the highest we've seen.) Nonverbal components of communication are HUGE. From tone to timing to context to location to body language, the whole package matters. That includes the communication medium (face-to-face, email, tweet, letter, phone, etc.). For church leaders, Matthew 7:12, Ephesians 4:15, and Philippians 2:3–4 offer clear guidance. The corollary temptation will be to discount nonverbal aspects of communication because those components are sometimes overstated.

We offer similar warnings regarding the complicated interactions of cultural, gender, and generational differences in communication. The more diverse the congregation, the more complex the communication process. Within some U.S. subcultures, "He wouldn't look me in the eye. I read that as deception," could be valid—though shame or guilt could be the real cause. Within other cultures, it is considered improper to make eye contact with persons who are older or of a higher rank in society. In the broadest of terms, women tend to reference their feelings more frequently and to describe them more fully than men.

Generationally speaking, we expect traditionalists to

be blunter than boomers; millennials are known for seeking consensus and valuing the feelings of others more than are boomers. Church leaders who are boomers from the corporate world may view communication as top-down (vertical and transactional) rather than friend-to-friend (primarily horizontal and relational). Generational differences are especially challenging for church leadership groups—elderships for example—that are generationally singular. If all elders fall within the same group, they may not know how differently other generational groups see the world and respond to it. It could be easy to think, "Our communication style has always worked for us; it should work for anybody." Servant-leaders won't expect others to do all the adjusting. Humility will foster flexibility. It will be in the nature of loving leaders to meet people far more than halfway.

We make no argument that every church leader must become expert in generational tendencies and peculiarities, that all communication challenges flow from generational differences, or that every member of any generation always follows his or her generational script. But knowing the major tendencies is wise. It frequently offers improved context for successful communication. It can keep us from talking at or past one another.

Myth 2

EFFECTIVE COMMUNICATION IS EASY.

W e wish we knew the origin of the encouraging proverb, "Communication is an art; become an artist." The gospels offer several examples of communication challenges. In John 2:18–23, Jesus (upon request) offered the Jews a sign of the veracity of His words: "Destroy this temple, and in three days I will raise it up." They "heard" Him to speak of a structure that took forty-six years to build, "but he was speaking about the temple of his body." Nicodemus fell victim to the same physical-versus-spiritual context in John 3:1–15. In the moment, he had no concept of a new spiritual birth. The woman at the well showed similar misunderstanding about living water and "... everyone who drinks of the water that I give will never be thirsty again" (John 4:13). All the apostles missed Jesus's use of "sleep" to mean "dead" in John 11:11–14. The Jews complained about Jesus's claim, "I am the bread of life" (John 6:35). "The Jews then disputed among themselves, saying, 'How can this man give us his flesh to eat?'" (John 6:52) Obviously, they missed the spiritual context of His teachings—and they were listening to the master teacher, the incarnate living word!

By inspiration, Peter acknowledged that Paul's letters included "some things ... that are hard to understand" (2 Pet 3:16). The Hebrew writer acknowledged major communication challenges with his initial audience (Heb 5:12–14). Paul tried to show the Corinthian Christians how they had misunderstood his previous letter to them (1 Cor 5:13).

For myriad reasons, communication often isn't easy! We write this as people who have tried to attend meetings both at the wrong times and on the wrong days. We once waited (impatiently) for a lunch date at the wrong McDonald's in a relatively small town. We live in a city— Florence, Alabama—that has an oversized post office because the plans were drawn for a facility in the notably larger Florence, South Carolina.

Assuming that communication either is—or should be—easy sets us up for failure and frustration. If communication, particularly with fellow Christians, is easy, then it shouldn't require much time and work. Planning and prayer aren't very important. There's no need to study the subject broadly within Scripture. There's no pull to keep learning better communication skills.

If communication is easy and it doesn't go well, then people must be purposefully thwarting the process. Satan loves this errant assertion because it moves communication challenges from the realm of human limitations to the realm of willful sin—self-will, lack of love, or disrespect for authority. If the devil gets us to believe that all major communication errors are intentional, then he has set us up to question and impugn the motives of others. He has set church leaders up to unfairly judge others. He has tempted us to accuse, attack, and sow discord among brethren (Prov 3:16–19).

Just because we've talked doesn't mean that people have listened. Just because they've listened doesn't mean that they've understood. It's far more than encoding and decoding or everybody being on the Lord's side. Quality communication touches every rail from context to history to fatigue to motivation to distraction to assumptions to expectations—and more.

In addition, group communication is infinitely more complicated than communication between individuals. That's true for communication within a group and flowing from a group. Every person in the room provides additional data. Did the yawn from the person in the third chair indicate dismissal, disinterest, or noisy neighbors the night before? Did silence from the person next to you mean approval, disapproval, a judgment that nothing needs to be said, or "I'm praying and weighing my words before speaking"? There's one easy recommendation: If you ever get the chance to take a course in group dynamics, take it!

Myth 3

COMMUNICATION SKILLS ARE INBORN.

P aul strongly indicates the opposite in 1 Corinthians 13:11: "When I was a child, I spoke like a child, I thought like a child, I reasoned like a child. When I became a man, I gave up childish ways." Likewise, the life of Moses opposes this myth. When Moses cited lack of eloquence as an excuse for rejecting God's commission, the Lord never disputed Moses's claim (Exod 4:10–17). Rather, He reminded Moses that He rules, creates, and empowers. He gave Moses a partner, saying of Aaron, "I know that he can speak well" (Exod 4:11). Our points? There's far more to effective communication than strong public speaking skills (2 Cor 10:10). More importantly, Moses's communication skills advanced impressively during the time he led Israel. We have no audio, but Moses's words from Deuteronomy 27–33 sing and soar. If communication was once not his strong suit, something changed for the better!

Life experience also argues that there's more to

communication skills than can be explained by DNA. Before we were blessed with our first son, I (Bill) thought all children were born "blank slate," that they came here with no programming and became what we made them. I knew I was wrong as soon as John was able to move and make sounds. When his brother, Allen, arrived some two years later, I realized that I had been STUNNINGLY wrong. Each boy arrived with his unique personality, preferences, and aptitudes.

Some are born with superior communication potential. Likely, some are born with a stronger tendency to value transparent, loving communication. Common sense says that communication flows more easily from extroverts than from introverts. But it would be a serious error to claim that communication skills are strictly a matter of nature (genetics). Nurture (social environment) also plays a major role. We'd never assert the ability to parse the respective roles of nature and nurture in the development of communication skills. Our best understanding is that the complex and dynamic interplay of nature and nurture continues to shape each of us throughout our lives.

Why would Satan tempt us to believe that communication skills are fully inborn? The devil knows that human brains are wired for basic logic. If communication skills are fully inborn, they can't be improved. If they can't be improved, there's no need to try—and God, rather than any individual, is responsible for any deficiencies. Satan wins BIG any time he keeps us from realizing that we can improve. He wins double if he leads us to believe that it's God who has purposefully placed us in such a poor position.

Communication skills can be improved with desire, study, and effort. For church leaders, we add prayer and God's blessing. Paul indicates this in 1 Timothy 4:11–16. He called Timothy to show evident public progress in speech, public reading of Scripture, exhortation, and teaching—all aspects of communication.

What is our recommendation in light of Satan's con that church leaders are either born with strong communication skills or they'll never have them? Prove him wrong. Study excellent communicators within Scripture —Moses, Joshua, David, Isaiah, Nehemiah, Paul, and especially Jesus. Identify skills, tendencies, and attitudes. Benefit from the literature of communication. Read advisedly, but read for both insight and motivation. Process—and invite others to help you process—your latest communication efforts and your personal communication style. "What's going well and helping me be a blessing? What's unclear, unsettling, inefficient, or off-putting?" Teach a course within the Bible school curriculum on Effective Communication According to the Bible. As you know, no one learns more than the teacher. If the class is interactive—and we can't imagine a communication course that isn't—it will work on multiple levels. People will learn more about communication, they'll practice their communication skills, and they'll do so with heightened awareness of assessing and improving. Not only will the course be energizing, it will also bless the congregation to see leaders working to improve.

Myth 4

CHURCH COMMUNICATION IS MORE
TRANSACTIONAL THAN RELATIONAL.

W e hear this myth in various forms. "The church needs to be run like a business." "If we did things in a business-like way, church life would sure be smoother." "Those who know what to do need to tell those who don't; and the ones being told need to listen."

While this claim sounds efficient, it misses several key points. The church is the body of Christ, and we are members—family, brothers, sisters—one of another (1 Cor 12, Eph 5:22–33). Christ-imitating love is a key identifying quality of the church (John 13:34–35). While it's good to follow God-honoring business practices, neither profit nor efficiency is our primary goal (Matt 6:19–22, Luke 9:23–26 & 12:15, 1 Tim 6:6–19). We love the description of the church as "a kingdom of right relationships," based on Ephesians 5:22–33. Our goal is to help one another live in Christ and become like Christ (Eph 4:11–16). We work both willingly and lovingly with flawed people (1 Thess 5:14) because the Lord works with us and our flaws.

We don't dispute the God-given authority of elders (1 Pet 5:1–5, Heb 13:7 & 17). There's a place for authoritative communication (Gal 2:11–21, Titus 1:10–16). We recognize, however, that even gospel truth must be spoken in love (Eph 4:15, 1 Thess 2:7–12). If it isn't, the method can hide or hinder the message. The passages cited here need to be read in balance. Considered with 1 Thessalonians 5:14, they remind every church leader not to use a hammer when a feather will do. It's not our job to put people in their place; our job is to call people to the heart and mission of Jesus.

Transactional communication has its place and its value. Nuance and subtlety don't count for much if the message is "The bridge is out!" In the grocery store, "Where can I find the canned beans?" doesn't require assorted pleasantries. But even at the grocery we appreciate the Publix difference. Transactional communication—just state the facts, don't invest great time in the feelings—has a place in the ebb and flow of church life. It becomes problematic when it's the primary mode of communication and when people are especially fragile. And we can't always see who's fragile in the moment.

Relational communication flows from respect. It affirms people's value to God (Gen 2:26–27). It sends the message, "God loves you, and we do, too." It's a little softer, a little sweeter, and a little nicer than it has to be. For a teacher, we ask, "Would you mind if I made a small suggestion about your fine class?" rather than saying, "Teacher, you're bugging the daylights out of me." For a single mom wrestling three young kids, we offer, "I so appreciate all the effort you're making to bring your children up in the Lord. You seem to be outnumbered. Would you mind if I sat with you to offer an extra set of hands?" rather than "Your unruly kids are causing a scene. You have to find a way to do better." For the little old lady who says to you, "You're sitting in my pew. I've been sitting there for 38 years. Everybody knows it's my pew," we try, "Yes ma'am, is the pew in front of you open?" rather than "We were here first today." And yes, that has happened to us—multiple times.

Relational communication is thoughtful in every sense of the word. "How can I use this opportunity to reflect the love of Jesus?" "How can we maximize the likelihood that God will be honored?" "What traps should we anticipate and avoid?" "How can my words best fit Proverbs 15:1 and 25:11–12?" "If he needed to say to me what I need to say to him, how would I want it said?" (Matt 7:12, Phil 2:3–4)

As Christians, our goal in communication is never just to get the job done. Our goal is to use every opportunity to encourage, bless, and build love.

Myth 5

A t first glance, Scripture might seem to support this statement. Within the family, parents are not to withhold correction from their children (Prov 13:24 & 23:13). The books of prophecy strongly emphasize God's correction of His sinful people (Isa 1, Jer 2, Ezek 2). The woes of Jesus recorded in Matthew 23 are scathing. Paul's epistles focus heavily on correction (1 Cor 1:10–15 & chapters 5–6, Gal 1:6–10, Col 2).

On balance, however, the wisdom literature offers more instruction and encouragement than correction. For all the fierce indictments, the prophets include major sections of encouragement and hope (Isa 40, Lam 3:19–33, Dan 2:44–45, Mic 6:8). Neither Paul nor Jesus could accurately be labeled as motivating primarily by scolding. While stoutly opposing spiritual rebellion and hypocrisy, they both consistently encouraged all who were seeking God's will. Jesus draws us through His love and sacrificial death (John 12:32). He offers us abundant life and a wondrous future (John 10:10 & 14:1–4). Paul began virtually every letter expressing love, hope, and gratitude. He also revisited each of those forms of encouragement at the end of most of his letters.

An example may help. Think of a difficult teen who has exasperated his poor parents. Everything he does seems purposefully wrong. In their pain and frustration, every word they speak to him seems harsh and scolding. Their teen comes to expect only criticism. His defensiveness shuts down both his ability and his willingness to hear his parents. No positive future exists within that cycle.

We know what the wise grandparents will suggest. We may even know how they'll say it.

> You guys know that we love you and always will. We can see and feel your pain. Could we offer a suggestion? You and your son need a fresh start. The negativity isn't working. Where things stand right now, he's immune to verbal correction—no matter how just or deserved it is. Can we ask you to try a different approach? Just for a while, don't scold. No matter how much effort it takes, catch him doing something good and say so. Surprise him with grace. It's the best way we know to push RESET and find a better way to try again. It's the ONLY way if you want a chance of maintaining any influence in his life."

Of course there's no guarantee of positive response even if the parents implement the soundest advice. Each individual holds the power of choice. Our point is not guaranteeing a result, but recommending the most biblical and engaging approach.

A familiar example demonstrates the power of an engaging approach. Remember the angel's word to Gideon: "The Lord is with you, O mighty man of valor" (Judg 6:11). Those words were not an accurate description of Gideon in real time; rather, they were prophetic, future-focused, and seed-planting. God called Gideon who he would become rather than who he was at the moment they met. In the very best sense of the phrase, the angel "talked Gideon up." We see hints of that same principle as Jesus described Peter in Matthew 16:13–19. We see more than hints in Ephesians 2:10, 2 Corinthians 8:22 and 9:1–2, and 1 Thessalonians 4:9–10. In each of these texts, the Holy Spirit had Paul use stunningly positive words to bring out the best in the brethren. It wasn't flattery or manipulation; rather it was faithful optimism flowing from the presence of Christ in their lives.

As mentioned earlier, there's clearly a place for reproof and correction, both in the family and in the church. But reproof and correction are not the primary communication pattern taught in Scripture. Over time, imbalanced communication that's focused on the negative tends to be heard only as mere background noise. At best it loses effect; at worst it rubs holes in relationships.

Faithful church leaders apply 2 Timothy 3:16–17 and 4:1–5 with love and courage, and they also remember that Ephesians 4:29 and Colossians 4:6 hold tremendous power. There are those who must be saved "by snatching them out of the fire" (Jude 20–23). Even then, we watch our motives and our approach (Gal 6:1–5). We can't rightly let ourselves impede God's work.

We have known a few church leaders who thought the ability to correct people with vigor and clarity was their God-given gift. Admittedly, they were good at it. They stayed in practice. In discussions, they were known to say, "Yes, the harder side of communication is my gift. I leave the encouraging stuff to others." We see no such division of labor in Scripture. We find it too dangerous, too easily misused, and too frequently misunderstood. The beauty of biblical balance is a stunningly safer course.

We reject the temptation to think that we can scold or "guilt" people into becoming more like Jesus. Spiritual transformation doesn't work that way. Life in a healthy church doesn't work that way. We're blessed to employ a fundamentally positive and encouraging communicational approach. We choose to model wisdom, self-examination, gentleness, and grace.

Myth 6

W e love the wisdom shown by God in ordaining that a plurality of elders leads His church (Acts 14:23, 1 Tim 3, Titus 1). Even in the absence of elders, it seems wise and proper that church leadership never becomes the domain of an individual. We recognize that the mechanics of how elders are to lead are not detailed within Scripture. The Bible speaks on the level of function and principle (Acts 20:28–32, 1 Tim 5:17–20, Heb 13:7 & 17, 1 Pet 5:1–5).

While the myth under discussion applies particularly to elders, it touches other leadership groups as well. For example, an eldership might prefer that the preacher— even though not an elder—serve as their spokesman. If work teams or committees are utilized, they may choose a spokesperson. Certainly, this is an area open to much flexibility and judgment.

A major danger is obvious, particularly for elderships. If the same elder is always the spokesman for the group, people will be tempted to see that elder as THE

ELDER. We're not speculating as to intent or judging motives; rather we're recognizing a strong human tendency. The voice and face of the group will be given disproportionate influence.

Why would any group choose a single spokesman? Sometimes it's based on seniority and flows from respect. "Wisdom is with the aged and understanding in length of days" (Job 12:12). It's interesting that the next paragraph extols God's wisdom and might as categorically superior to anything humans could claim. The older we get, the more we respect both age and wisdom. And the older we get, the more we realize that age doesn't always bring wisdom. Think of Psalm 90:10–12; the connection between wisdom and age isn't automatic. Think of the twin stories in 1 Kings 12–13. In chapter 12, the young men are foolish and the old men wise. In chapter 13, the lie of the old prophet causes a young prophet to sin and die.

Sometimes the choice of spokesperson isn't about age or wisdom; it's about appearance, charisma, or public speaking ability. None of these blessings are evil. People prefer communication from those who are personable, pleasant, and skilled. A natural question arises: "How can those who are not yet skilled develop skill if they don't get opportunity to practice?" Major concerns come to mind. If one skilled person is always the spokesman, what happens if he moves or dies? The next man up needs to be ready. Might the devil try to use the spokesman role to plant questions about disproportionate influence or to tempt that spokesman to pride?

Charisma and eloquence can be tremendous blessings. Think of Apollos (Acts 18:24–28). On the other hand, Absalom, who had a tremendous ability to influence people, used his talent to undermine his father's kingship (2 Sam 15:1–13). Remember the smooth-as-oil communication skills of the temptress as described in Proverbs 5:3. Moses, arguably the greatest Old Testament leader, needed Aaron's help with public speaking. Paul stoutly rejected the concept of viewing rhetorical ability and human wisdom as the foundations of his gospel ministry (1 Cor 1:18–31). Charisma and eloquence are never, in themselves, signs of evil or deceit. Nor are they, in themselves, evidence of truth and wisdom.

What do we recommend to church leaders? There's safety and wisdom in turn-taking. Sometimes, the brother who has to work hardest at public communication packs the biggest punch. People identify with his struggle and admire his godly effort. We've heard people say, "If he can try so hard outside his comfort zone, maybe I need to do more myself." And we love the message sent when more able and experienced brothers encourage newer leaders to serve as spokesmen. Without a word, they can tell the church how they function as elders: "We are a team of equals under the lordship of Christ. Each of us is willing to step up and do our best. We're not a group that judges one another based on current level of confidence and skill. We gladly work with God as He makes each of us better." What we do and how we do it communicates just as importantly as what we say. These opportunities are too valuable to miss.

Myth 7

HISTORY DOESN'T INFLUENCE CURRENT COMMUNICATION.

or humans, the past is never fully past. We love
Paul's beautiful language from Philippians
3:13–14:

> Brothers, I do not consider myself to have
> made it my own. But this one thing I do:
> forgetting what lies behind and straining
> forward to what lies ahead, I press on toward
> the goal for the prize of the upward call of
> God in Christ Jesus."

We love the gospel language of 2 Corinthians 5:17:
"Therefore, if anyone is in Christ, he is a new creation.
The old has passed away; behold, the new has come."

Both passages are powerfully true. Dying and rising
with Christ (Rom 6:4) utterly changed Paul's attitude
and perspective toward his former conduct with
Judaism. He moved from persecutor to preacher of the
gospel. His mission and his methods radically changed as

he took on the commission of preaching the gospel to every creature.

Without compromising the truth of Philippians 3 or 2 Corinthians 5, we can also say without hesitation that Paul never completely forgot his past—not in the sense of erasing memory or failing to remember the lessons he had learned. Scripture says as much (Acts 26:1–23, 1 Cor 15:9–10). He reframed his past in light of knowing the resurrected Jesus. Persecution—that he once deemed righteous and patriotic—he now saw as harmful to people and wrong before God. The once lofty goal of advancing within Judaism no longer held any value. All of his life was now devoted to knowing, loving, and serving Christ.

The devil would use our past against us. He'd have us label ourselves as unforgivable. If that fails, he moves to "You're too damaged by your past to be of any use to God. You're permanently shackled by shame." If necessary, he will take the opposite tact; he'll tempt with delusion. "Forget your past. In fact, God commands you to forget your past—it has nothing to offer you anyway." Trying to forget our past is like trying not to think of a flying pink elephant. The very act of telling ourselves not to remember ensures that we do.

Because communication is relational, it always has a history. This is true on multiple levels. Each of us has communicational habits and preferences. At times, we revert to our default settings—and we may not even realize that we've done so. (Have you ever said something a little sharp or snarky and immediately asked yourself, "Where did THAT come from?")

Even in our first conversation with a new-to-us

person, he may remind us of someone we know—or we may remind her of someone who has caused notable pain. This, too, can happen at a subconscious level. We don't quite know what's wrong, but something's awkward and uneasy.

When communicating with people we know, the history may be more obvious and impactful. Positively, what a joy to think, "This person has always been straight and fair with me. I can trust him. He reminds me of Nathanael" (John 1:47). On the other hand, how challenging to know, "Warning. Caution. This person tends to twist words and tell tales. I don't want to be burned again." And there's a huge, complicated territory between these examples.

Communication history becomes ever more complex when groups are involved. Why might an eldership exclude the preacher from virtually all of its meetings? Chances are that the answer flows from history. Why might an eldership choose never to meet with the whole church just to listen? It's likely that something went poorly in the past. Why might a brother seem hyper-defensive when faced with a question? It's possible that previous pain has taught him to always look for the hook.

In view of the ongoing power of the past, we recommend self-awareness and self-assessment. Why do certain communication settings come with high anxiety? If I start feeling angry or anxious, how will I stay in control and act better than I feel? When I've felt this way in the past, how have I responded? Were my responses Christ-like? Are better options available? In what ways do I need God's help in this moment?

Myth 8

A n even more damaging version of this myth is "Use the tool you prefer, even if the right one is available." We sometimes hear it tragically stated as "I know what the Bible says, but ... ." How does this apply to communication and church leaders?

The Bible mandates that some communication be handled person-to-person, one-on-one (Matt 18:15–20). We see the wisdom in this instruction. It's nimble, requiring minimal scheduling and allowing maximum flexibility. It minimizes the impact of egos; there's no audience tempting anyone to save face. It fits the Golden Rule (Matt 7:12). It encourages us to be our brother's keeper (Phil 2:3–4). It's loving (1 Cor 13:4–8, John 13:34–35). It shows courage and invites trust.

Given those virtues, why isn't the tool of one-on-one, face-to-face communication employed more often? It doesn't always feel comfortable. It involves risk; it can go tragically wrong. It's not normal in this sin-damaged world. "Normal" in the fog of sin is recruiting allies and choosing to talk to everyone except the person with whom we need to speak first.

The devil will help us "see" reasons that the situation at hand is an exception to Matthew 18:15. To be fair, there are exceptions, as made clear by Galatians 2:11–21. Peter sinned before all and endangered the unity of the church. The correction needed to be as public as the sin. Peter acted publicly and intentionally in a way he knew to be wrong. We must be very careful, however. Even when Apollos publicly taught an incomplete gospel, Aquila and Priscilla still "took him aside and explained to him the way of God more accurately" (Acts 18:26). Evidently, motive and intent matter. A person erring in ignorance is categorically different from a person erring through hypocrisy. We'll certainly need God's help with discernment (Jas 1:5, Heb 5:14).

The devil doesn't care which ditch he pulls us into. Right or left, it's still a ditch, and it's off the path. It's no better to handle a private matter publicly than to endanger the health of the church in the name of sparing feelings and protecting reputations.

Within churches, a classic example of using the wrong tool is speaking from the pulpit when we should be talking privately. We love church leaders who diligently resist this temptation. We know preachers and elders who practice loving caution by offering a private heads-up when there's even a small danger that a sermon or class could be seen as misuse of power. What does that look like? "John, you know we've been studying through 1 Corinthians. We'll be in chapter 6 on Sunday. I just wanted to offer a heads-up that this class in no way flows from the fact that your neighbor recently sued you. I don't do business that way, and I don't even want to look like I do." In a sense, we see this as inexpensive insurance—it prevents a potential problem. More importantly, it's a wonderful application of Hebrews 10:24. It puts us on the record as working to have good hearts.

Another application of choosing to use the right tool involves attention to people's communication preferences. There are advantages to letters for those who still read and practice old-school niceties. Letters offer chances for reflection and improving levels of reception. (Sometimes our first reaction isn't our best.) Letters can be read by a trusted friend and softened before they're sent. But receiving a letter can be an insult if a visit was expected.

Some don't mind an email, text, or tweet. Our rule of thumb with these—and with letters—is simple: Write as if your communication will be the lead story on the local news tomorrow night. Stay nice, kind, and respectful. Even when—especially when—highly provoked, avoid gigs and digs. Take the high road every time. The one time we don't, Satan will pounce.

A classic rule of interpersonal communication states, "You can always add to your words, but you can never get them back." Whenever Scripture and common sense allow, we start soft and light. We can always say more later if more needs to be said. We don't tell when we can ask. We invite and encourage rather than order and demand. If I need to smite the mosquito on your arm, an eight-pound hammer isn't the tool to use.

Jesus consistently used the best communication tool for the job at hand. To the devil, He quoted Scripture

(Matt 4). To those willing to listen, He taught exten-sively (Matt 5–7). To those whose faith merited praise, He offered generous compliment (Matt 8:4–13). To those who needed to do more thinking, He provided food for thought (Matt 8:18–22). When hearts needed to be chal-lenged, He challenged hearts (Matt 9:1–8). When evidence was needed, He invited people to come and see (Matt 11:1–6). When right to do so, He could rebuke with vigor and clarity (Matt 11:20–37 and chapter 23). When illustrations served better than commands, He offered the greatest of stories (Matt 13). When He knew that a challenge would offer faith the chance to shine, He offered the opportunity without hesitation (Matt 15:21–28).When crucial choice needed to be made, Jesus made that choice crystal clear (Matt 19:16–22). When a trap question deserved no answer, He turned the tables and upped the challenge (Matt 20:23–27). When a conversation needed to be elevated, He took it right out of this world (Matt 22:15–22). And when nothing needed to be said, "he gave him no answer, not even to a single charge" (Matt 27:13–14).

In everything Jesus remains THE Master and THE example. With communication, He employed the right tool at the right time in the right manner every time. And even with the extensive list above, the half has not been told.

Myth 9

SOME SUBJECTS ARE PERMANENTLY OFF LIMITS.

As noted in Myth 8, not every question merits an answer. Following Jesus's example sometimes means answering a better question than the one that's put before us. We don't want to be baited into conversations that harm rather than help. On the level of principle, 2 Timothy 2:23 offers solid counsel: "Have nothing to do with foolish, ignorant controversies; you know that they breed quarrels." Clearly, there is "a time to keep silence and a time to speak" (Eccl 3:7, Prov 17:27–28). There's a time for talk and a time for action. Nehemiah famously rejected the "offer of communication" trap that enemies laid for him (Neh 6:1–9). With God's help, he saw through the ruse. His stated reason for refusing the meeting is classic: "I am doing a great work and I cannot come down" (Neh 6:3).

Quick responses aren't always the best responses (Prov 29:20). There are even God-given truths that people are not yet able to hear (John 16:12, Heb 5:12–14).

In such situations, it's wise to bide our time and hold our tongues.

We're blessed to honor those facts while also remembering Acts 20:26–27, where Paul says to the Ephesian elders, "Therefore I testify to you this day that I am innocent of the blood of all, for I did not shrink from declaring to you the whole counsel of God." In doing so, he was honoring the commission of Jesus, "teaching them to observe all that I have commanded you" (Matt 28:20). Concerning the doctrine of Christ, we're to love, live, and teach the truth, the whole truth, and nothing but the truth.

The devil would love to convince church leaders that some subjects—even some directly biblical subjects—are better left alone. "We live in polarized and hyper-sensitive times. Don't dare speak of race relations or social justice." "Matthew 19:1–9 is stunningly controversial in some settings; it's best not to go there." "Teaching from Romans 13 could get us into politics and church-state relations. That's just too hot to handle." The devil loves to cast aspersions at God's revelation. He loves the shadows and doubts created by gaps in teaching. He knows what tends to grow in those shadows. And we're blessed to teach the whole of Scripture in faith and love. Biblical subjects can't be off limits for the people of the Book.

There's another version of the "some subjects are permanently off limits" myth. It deals with matters of policy, procedure, and protocol. "When the congregation gets ready to add elders, will members be encouraged to submit names?" "Would the elders welcome suggestions and discussion of new outreach efforts?"

"Could we explore offering a community course on parenting skills on Tuesday evenings?" "When a member wants to offer a suggestion for improvement, what's the best way to do that?"

Satan would love to see church leaders view such questions defensively. "Why is **he** asking that **now**? What's the agenda? What's really going on? Why is our leadership being questioned?" Good people love leaders who welcome input. Good people love leaders who assume the best of motives until proven otherwise. Good people love leaders who welcome opportunity for engagement and improvement. Good people love leaders who know that truth never fears inquiry.

When leaders are asked, "Can we talk about ____?" the fundamental answer is a happy yes. Being open to and available for conversation is a position of major strength. Yes, there are exceptions. As noted previously, Jesus's critics laid frequent traps. But Jesus never came to view every question as a trap—or even as an obstacle. One could argue that He viewed every question—even the ones He didn't answer—as an opportunity to teach. Wise church leaders refuse to hide, even from challenging questions.

Myth 10

TIMING IN COMMUNICATION IS NO BIG DEAL.

W hy would we think any church leader would believe this myth? Regrettably, examples abound. A congregation learns "backdoor" through social media that their new preacher has been hired. The elders were going to tell them "once all the details were finalized." VBS was cancelled due to COVID, but there was no announcement until the week before. "The retirement reception honoring our beloved church secretary of thirty years has been scheduled for 2:00 on Mother's Day afternoon." There are many levels of timing errors.

The book of Esther offers a clinic on the value of timely communication. Whether from amazing wisdom or instruction from God, Mordecai instructed Esther to keep her Jewish roots secret (Esth 2:8–11). We don't learn why that matters until later in the story, but premature communication could have cost Esther the opportunity to help rescue God's people. In an amazing case of providence, King Ahasuerus is read the chronicle of a plot to kill him being foiled by Mordecai, and that reading occurred at a crucial time in the unfolding events (Esth 6:1–3). Esther herself provides the clearest evidence of the power of superbly timed communication. When offered up to half the kingdom, her only request was that the king and Haman dine with her (Esth 5:6–8). It was at the second meal, a day later and after the king had been reminded of Mordecai's life-saving action, that Esther deftly exposed Haman's evil plot (Esth 7). The context and timing of Esther's revelation turned the tide and saved the day.

Proverbs 25:11–12 hints at the importance of timely communication. "A word fitly spoken" speaks of communication that is clear, loving, appropriate, and timely. The watchman section of Ezekiel 33 emphasizes a warning that is clear, timely, and potentially lifesaving. Brethren have long noted the precise timing of God's ultimate communication with humanity: "But when the fulness of time had come, God sent forth his Son, born of woman, born under the law, to redeem those who were under the law, so that we might receive adoption as sons" (Gal 4:4–5).

Timing and timeliness impact church communication on many levels. Scripture supports the practice of maximum encouragement—sharing good news as soon as is possible (Luke 2:8–20, 15:5–10 & 22–23; Acts 14:26–27). Though the news was not to be good, remember how David longed for an immediate report about Absalom's safety (2 Sam 18:19–32). When people desire and expect news, delay is not welcome. If the delay is found to be purposeful, trust is damaged. And Satan invites the worst of interpretations. "They didn't love us enough to tell us." "They don't deem us worthy to be told." "They didn't even think of us."

Sometimes communication delays flow from pain— we delay telling difficult or disappointing news. We want to spare feelings for as long as possible. And we know the folly of such thinking in the age of instant communication. The operative question is not, "Can we make this less bad by delaying the telling?" The key question is, "Is it better for those we love to hear it from a trusted leader or from some random source?"

Communication delays can come from embarrassment. What must be communicated looks bad and feels bad because it is bad. Other delays flow from perfectionism. "We'll share this message with the church just as soon as we get it right. We can't share it until it's right." We love the desire to do our best for God. We also know that humans seldom do anything perfectly. We want to be sure of accuracy, attitude, and tone. But we also know the famous phrase "paralysis of analysis." We can lose the moment by trying to get the moment just right.

When communication doesn't happen in a timely manner, several dynamics change. Rather than looking transparent and gracious, we can appear to be petty and withholding. We can come to look like we communicated unwillingly, only because we were forced to. When difficult news must be shared, take reasonable time to pray and think, but value the word *reasonable*. Playing catch up with communication is never easy or pleasant.

Myth 11

BECAUSE I KNOW WHAT I MEAN, YOU KNOW WHAT I MEAN.

W hen teaching the importance of context, the limitations of language, and the danger of assumptions, we love The Box Sequence. We offer our class a communication exercise. "We're going to give you a statement. Without consulting with anyone, write on your paper what comes next." And the statement we provide is "I will box them for you."

Assuming the context of a floral shop, what comes next is the florist puts the long-stemmed red roses into a lovely box. Assuming a landscaper standing by a row of unruly shrubs, what comes next is that he trims the plants into perfect neatness. Assuming a hero in a classic movie rescuing a damsel in distress, what happens next is the bad guys get a lesson in the school of hard knocks. The key word is assuming—without context, communication fails.

Even among the best of people, context is often missed. As Hannah poured out her heart to God, Eli assumed she was drunk and scolded her (1 Sam 1:12–16).

As David asked about Goliath—and admittedly the reward for slaying the giant, his brother Eliab assumed an ignoble motive and offered stinging rebuke (1 Sam 17:26–30). When a Samaritan village asked Jesus to move on, James and John knew just what was needed. They asked permission from Jesus to call down consuming fire from heaven (Luke 9:51–56). Despite all His teaching and all the time they had spent with Jesus, they had yet to grasp the core of His mission (John 3:17, Matt 20:28).

Challenges multiply when we try to communicate across cultures, generations, and value systems. Remember the young man who assumed he would be rewarded for bringing David news of the deaths of Saul and his sons (2 Sam 1). His claim to have killed David's persecutor led to his own execution. When King David thoughtfully sent emissaries to Hanun, new king of Ammon, Hanun's advisors assumed they were spies, dishonored them, and started a small war (2 Sam 10). They were unwilling to believe that David's gifts were meant to show support for a grieving fellow ruler.

We don't want to make the cynical claim that what can be misunderstood will be misunderstood, but cynics sometimes have a point. A hyper-keeper of the Sabbath assumed that even Jesus was not allowed to do a miracle of healing on the day of rest (Luke 13:10–17). Magnificent mercy was mislabeled as disregard for God's law. The message of the miracle was missed by those who showed no mercy. Such people would find the father of the prodigal soft-headed and present the ungracious elder brother as both the victim and the unsung hero of that story (Luke 15:11–32). May God save us from horrible thinking!

"Because I know what I mean, you know what I mean" comes with several corollaries. The most insidious sub-myth continues the line with "so I have no need to explain myself. Either you get it or you don't. I owe you no help." An equally dangerous version says, "If you don't catch my meaning, it's intentional. You've chosen to be my enemy." A more pragmatic version assumes, "If you don't catch my meaning, then you weren't meant to understand. I'll let this be and let the chips fall where they may."

A different level of deceptive corollary reasons, "It's your job to catch my meaning, whether or not I make it clear." A darker version reads, "You're obligated to catch my intended meaning no matter what I say." These assertions won't fly biblically (Matt 5:37, Jas 3:8–12). Throughout Scripture, God sets an outstanding example of going the second and third miles to make His message and meaning clear. Think of the purposeful repetition within the Old Testament, the inclusion of four gospel accounts within the New Testament, and the amazing parallels within the epistles (Rom 12:3–8 and 1 Cor 12, Eph 4:17–5:21 and Col 3, 1 Tim 3 and Titus 1:5–9).

We love the common-sensical adage: Communicate, communicate, and re-communicate. When you think the message is unmistakably clear, perhaps you have begun to communicate. We cringe at the cynical adage: If you want information to be unclear, announce it in the assembly. If you want it completely forgotten, put it in the church bulletin. We cringe because we have seen it happen.

Myth 12

I KNOW WHAT YOU MEAN, EVEN BEFORE YOU TELL ME.

This close cousin of Myth 11 immediately turns our minds to Proverbs 18:13, "If one gives an answer before he hears, it is his folly and shame." Only God is able to accurately discern people's meaning before their thoughts and words are formed (Ps 139:1–4). Though people know this on a logical level, it's often forgotten in our daily interactions.

We recently watched a TV game show. The big brain participant buzzed before the host finished reading the question, and he missed the answer. He knew the subject and the details, but he made an errant guess about the ending of the question. The studio audience roared with laughter. But it's never funny when this happens to us or we do it to others.

There's fundamental linkage between quality listening and respect, fairness, humility, patience, and self-discipline. Respect for others originates in respect for God (Gen 2:26–27, Ps 8). Because God chooses to love and value each person, we do too (John 3:16, Mark 16:15).

The Golden Rule demands fundamental fairness on our part (Matt 7:12). We are not arguing that life is always fair or that we'd be better off if it were (Rom 3:23, 6:23). Rather, we propose that choosing to treat others with fundamental fairness is wise, virtuous, and biblically-supported (Rom 12:10–13, 1 Cor 13:4–8, Eph 4:25–32).

James 1:19–20 powerfully links listening with humility, patience, and self-discipline. Many of us are not naturally "quick to hear, slow to speak, slow to anger." Even if we do well with anger, we still find ourselves wanting our turn to speak somewhat before it becomes available. Humility waits. Humility informs and empowers patience. "I want to show respect. I don't want to bully or run ahead. If I wait and listen, things will go better. I don't have to be first or loudest." Applied as a package, humility and patience grow in the spiritual virtue of self-control (Gal 5:22–26).

We've spoken from the perspective of showing humility and patience toward the people with whom we communicate as church leaders, but there's far more to the issue. The greatest humility and patience is that which we show toward God. God says to listen lovingly and graciously (Prov 18:13, Col 4:5–6). We show tremendous wisdom and self-control when we choose to believe and obey God.

We know the "tape" that the devil would have us play. "If I listen too long, they'll get the upper hand. If I listen too long, I'll forget what I planned to say. If I listen too long, the moment will pass. If I listen too long, I'll seem slow or ignorant. If I don't stand up for myself, nobody will." We also know the biblical tape. "Be quick to hear and slow to speak. Keep all emotions in check. Listen and learn. Christ has blessed me to wear His name. I must always live up to that name. God is in control. If I do things God's way, God will bless." Bottom line, it's an issue of trust. Who can take better care of us, ourselves or our God?

In fairness, we do sometimes know what others mean even before they tell us. It's a combination of some people being highly predictable, our gaining wisdom over years, and being blessed to read the room effectively. Even when we already know what others mean, it's still a blessing to let them explain. It's still humble and patient. It's also strategic. It sets a tone of respect and self-control. It models virtues that God would have us model. It demonstrates servant leadership and accrues leadership credits in the hearts of those who watch it happen. While accruing credits is never the goal, it's often a serendipity that God provides in His infinite goodness.

Myth 13

MY WORDS MEAN EXACTLY AND ONLY
WHAT I MEAN THEM TO MEAN.

At every level, human language is stunningly complex—remember The Box Sequence from Myth 11. "Fly up to the office and bring back my calendar" holds quite a different meaning if the office is in Toronto rather than on the second floor of the building in which we're currently standing. In one case, we need the corporate jet. In the other, *fly* is a creative way to say *hurry*.

In a church setting people expect clear, honest, and transparent communication. They don't expect to be misled or manipulated. Jesus thwarted the communication games played by the devil—games that included quotations from Scripture (Matt 4). Jesus stoutly condemned the communication games played by the religious leaders of His day (Matt 23). The deck was stacked toward the people in the know. Swearing by the temple was nothing; the oath counted only if it mentioned the gold in the temple. Swearing by the altar was nothing; the oath held power only if it referenced the gift on the altar. Jesus had no use for such deception.

In light of Matthew 23, we dare not present a dismissal meeting as a performance review. We dare not schedule a meeting where one person gets to prepare but the other feels ambushed. We dare not present an involuntary change as voluntary—or a unilateral decision as a mutual agreement. Church leaders know to do better. We dare not say, "Get this done," only to add later, "You know we meant 'get this done when the time is right so it won't raise concerns.'"

As church leaders, we are blessed never to hide behind our words. Satan must love the sorry episode of Genesis 27:29–36. After shredding Joseph's robe and staining it with goat's blood, Joseph's brothers "brought it to their father and said, 'This we have found; please identify whether it is your son's robe or not.'" Their first statement was a lie, but—in the eyes of the world—only a small lie. The second was a dodge, a "conscience salver." It allowed them to say to themselves, "We never actually said that Joseph was dead. We just framed the matter to our advantage and let Dad draw his own conclusions. What followed isn't our fault." What they did was cold, cruel, and not half as clever as they imagined.

We dare not follow the example of Joseph's brothers, but we will be tempted. "Drive the church van during the week to keep the battery charged" can't rightly become "Of course we meant that you should drive it only for official church business." "You're welcome to exercise flexibility in your schedule" can't fairly mutate to include "as long as you check with us and get advance approval." "Please take care of that need" can't righteously become "We meant for you to take care of it as much as was possible without spending any funds."

What are we recommending? As church leaders, communicate as clearly and fairly as possible. Learn from every communication glitch. How much of this is on us? Were we too generic? Did we assume too much? How can we do better next time? Assume the best motives in others, but if honest assessment says, "At least to some degree, we've been played," establish clearer communication. Be more detailed and specific. Build in better safeguards for next time.

Clearly, two contradictory categories are in play. One flows from human limitations: Miscommunication happens. The other, however, flows from human manipulation: We try to avoid conflict or maximize control by using words in non-standard or misleading ways. And, in either situation, the devil delights when he can get us to meet him on his terms.

A CAVEAT

As surely as church leaders can use words in ways that are "unique" and misleading, any person can choose to hear unfairly. We do well to communicate to the best of our ability using biblical terms and principles according to their time-honored meanings. Even when we do, people will sometimes assume non-standard (idiosyncratic) meanings that never crossed our minds. There's little way to anticipate such purposeful mishearing. All we know to recommend is to challenge such choices kindly, directly, and lovingly. Godly communication depends on mutual good faith effort. Anything less gives place to the tempter.

Myth 14

THE LESS MOST PEOPLE KNOW, THE BETTER.

Satan loves effusive communication when the words include lie, gossip, rumor, slander, and discouragement. But when good words flow from good hearts, he becomes a minimalist. The devil grasps human psychology. He knows that people love to be included and informed. They love to be considered.

God knows this, too. We see God sharing extra information with His friend Abraham (Gen 18:16–21). We see God giving volumes of information to and through His prophets. We hear Jesus affirming the principle of forthcoming communication in John 15:14–15:

> You are my friends if you do what I command you. No longer do I call you servants, for the servant does not know what his master is doing; but I have called you friends, for all that I have heard from my Father I have made known to you."

Acts 6:1–7 offers a classic example of collaborative church leadership where the problem at hand is publicly stated, the leaders propose a solution, the people are asked to help implement the solution, and major church growth follows. Philippians 4:10–20 and 1 Thessalonians 2:1–12 both document major personal disclosures from Paul in service to the gospel. He shared his heart and his struggles to bless the brethren and to prepare them for struggles of their own. We read Paul's ultimate self-disclosures in 2 Corinthians 11–12, Philippians 3:1–16, and 2 Timothy 4:6–8. In each case, he modeled courageous forthcoming communication by a godly leader.

We are not advocating the foolish extreme of "everybody always has the right to know everything." Trumpeting that extreme is a major way that Satan attacks efforts toward healthy transparency. He presents the blessed transparency of healthy communication as a slippery slope from which there is no escape.

People tend to behave badly in the absence of facts. They invent and impugn motives. They create alternate realities that seem to make sense once a few foundational errors are accepted. This is NOT a criticism of God, but when Abram and Sarai had to wait longer than expected for Isaac, they formulated a terrible plan to "help God out" (Gen 16). When Moses was on Sinai longer than expected, Israel hatched one of the Bible's all time worst plots (Exod 32).

To be fair, the Bible includes examples where excessive information was shared—and caused great harm. Joseph may have said too much when he shared his dreams with his jealous brothers (Gen 37). King Hezekiah unintentionally invited the Babylonian invasions by showing Nebuchadnezzar's envoy all the treasures of God's house (Isa 39). Peter definitely revealed too much of his heart when he rebuked the Lord (Matt 16:21–23).

On the other hand, why might church leaders be tempted to withhold information from the brethren? In keeping with Myth 7, some have shared important information in the past, and things didn't go well. People may have over-shared or prematurely shared information that should have been discussed only within the church. For some leaders, it's a matter of following the practices of beloved mentors. On the darker side, knowledge is power, and some choose to hoard power. We are wise to check our motives and our practices. Do they reflect the spirit and teaching of Jesus?

For some church leaders, the matter is much simpler than the paragraph above. Sometimes we don't share information because we don't know how. There's neither flaw nor shame in ignorance. The problem comes when we settle—when we choose to stay ignorant. Resources abound for those who are ready to learn. Adventure awaits those willing to launch out prayerfully. No matter how helpful the secular or human resources might be, God remains the Master Teacher. He will teach when our hearts are ready.

Myth 15

TO LISTEN IS TO AGREE.

T he power of this myth lies in its simplicity: "If a church leader listens to a person's viewpoint, then he has, at the minimum, given credence to that viewpoint." The stronger form asserts that the leader has tacitly approved or validated that view just by listening to it.

As noted in Myth 9, there are times NOT to listen (Neh 6:1–9, 2 Tim 2:29). Titus 1:10–16 speaks of "insubordinate, empty talkers, and deceivers" who upset whole families by teaching "what they ought not to teach." Paul says of these false teachers, "They must be silenced." In such cases, we can accurately say "to listen is to allow." Church leaders bless the body by accurately applying—but never over-applying—that principle.

Scripture offers many examples disproving the myth that to listen is to agree. God listened to Adam and Eve after their sin (Gen 3). Then, He passed righteous judgment. God listened to Cain's lament and responded with a mark of protection, but He did not alter His condemnation of Cain's sin (Gen 4). Moses listened to Aaron's pitiful excuse-making about the golden calf, but he didn't buy a word of it (Exod 32). Jesus often listened to His critics, but the gospels offer no example of the Savior being persuaded by their arguments.

We remember a classically bad explanation of refusing to listen in a church setting. There was disagreement over some minor matter of judgment. Many wanted further discussion, but a strong-minded church leader did not. His approach to closing communication was two-pronged. "First, God hates 'one who sows discord among brothers' (Prov 6:19). If we keep taking about this, discord will result. We're done talking." "Second, in my Bible 1 Thessalonians 5:22 says 'Abstain from all appearance of evil.' Talking about this matter looks like conflict and disunity. It's not right to keep talking." With all due respect to the Authorized Version, a fairer reading of the verse is, "Abstain from every form of evil." Our strong-willed brother failed to realize that he had declared any further discussion to be a form of evil—but many good people didn't agree.

Rather than "to listen is to agree," we propose that to listen is to learn, to love, to show respect, and to build bridges. We make no claim that even world-class listening always leads to harmony. More modestly, we suggest that biblically-guided listening offers the best path to trust, unity, and understanding. We think of the principle taught in Romans 12:18: "If possible, as far as it depends on you, live peaceably with all." Peace isn't always possible because multiple people are involved—it doesn't depend only on us. The same is true of the results of loving listening. We can make the effort, but the outcome is never fully ours to determine.

If we anticipate Satan's next ploy, he is likely to ask, "Then why try? Why extend the courtesy and make the effort when there's no guarantee that listening will lead to the best biblical outcome?" There are several solid answers. We listen to others because God graciously listens to us. Imitating our Father is always solid. We listen to others because we want others to listen to us. We love to apply the Golden Rule. We listen to others because God still changes minds and hearts. If we can play even a small role in God's work of making people more like Jesus, what a blessing! We listen to others because there is no good alternative.

And we listen to others because the potential rewards greatly outweigh the potential risks. Yes, some may mistakenly think that, because we listen, we agree with everything that's being said. Most will see the fallacy. Most will know that better reasons exist. And when in doubt, the fair-minded will ask us—just like we'd be fair and ask them.

Myth 16

We're amazed that some within church settings seem to believe all communication efforts are fundamentally the same, especially efforts that flow from official church leaders to the membership. In our best thinking, there are at least three types of group communication meetings.

We have seen wise church leaders effectively employ listening meetings. Some have been thematic—focused on a major issue or two. Others have been open-ended. Fundamentally, such meetings begin with prayer followed by, "We're here this evening to hear from you. While we can't promise that we can implement every idea that's suggested, we value your input. We want to know what you're thinking. We want to know what you want us to know." To make notes as brethren talk is both excellent optics (it sends the right visual message) and strategic (it's helpful to have a written record). We cannot over-emphasize how much most people appreciate the opportunity to be heard. It's amazing how often excellent ideas flow from such meetings.

Listening meetings will not happen where Myth 15 holds sway. They will not happen when trust is low or when tension is high. Listening meetings carry a degree of risk, but the upside is tremendous. They flow from love, humility, and a "one another" spirit within the church's leaders. And they support and build those same qualities among those being listened to.

A second type of group communication is the informational meeting. In some respects it's illustrated by Acts 14:27, where Paul and Barnabas reported to their sending church "all that God had done with them." We're not asserting that the mission team did no listening, just that the meeting's primary purpose was presenting a report, a targeted sharing of information. People love to be kept in the loop. For many fine people, the more they feel informed, the harder they work and the more happily they serve.

A third broad type of group communication is a decision-making meeting. The Jerusalem Conference of Acts 15 offers an example. While that meeting dealt with a major issue and involved many congregations, it offers principles that can bless less complex situations. Acts 15 documents fearless examination of the issue at hand, good-faith dialog between Christians who did not yet see eye to eye, and a foundational commitment to apply God's truth faithfully. The brethren did not run from conflict and challenge. They honored God by dealing lovingly with one another. And Paul, James, and others set outstanding examples of servant leadership.

Of course you see a flaw in the descriptions above.

To phrase the question biblically, "Given your three broad types of meetings, where does Acts 6:1–7 fall?" That meeting included characteristics from each of the types we've suggested. More than that, it was also a decision implementation meeting. No list of categories offered by humans is flawless or without overlap.

Why the emphasis on meeting types? What's the trap? We have seen the key trap in multiple settings. A listening meeting is announced and promoted, but a telling meeting occurs. A decision-making meeting is described and expected, but the group soon realizes that the decision has already been made and the purpose of the meeting is totally informational. When such happens, people feel disappointed and deceived. In such situations we've heard the term "bait and switch." Trust is violated, communication channels are poisoned, and relationships are damaged. It may seem like a small matter to those making the switch, but "a little leaven leavens the whole lump" (1 Cor 5:6). When it comes to trust and credibility, there are no little matters. We must never let the devil play us this way.

A CAVEAT

What if one type of meeting was announced in all good conscience, but the situation changed dramatically and a notably different meeting is now in order? Please don't ignore the elephant in the room. Be upfront. State the obvious from the start. "As you know, we invited you here for a listening meeting. There have been major developments, and we—as church leaders—had to make some challenging decisions. We need to share those decisions with you." Even if brethren are disappointed, they will respect courage and honesty.

Without such disclosure, the devil will seize the moment: "You've been played—and it's not the first time! I told you that you couldn't trust these people. You know what Jesus thinks of deceit. They said one thing but did another. That can't be right." No, it can't, but we can make every effort to put things right—even as things change in the most unpredictable of ways.

Myth 17

A BIT OF DECEPTION IS INEVITABLE, EXPECTED, HARMLESS, AND MAYBE EVEN BENEFICIAL.

W e're wise to be extremely cautious with this myth as Satan spins it in every possible way. To those with hypersensitive consciences, he'll say, "You know that you lied when you didn't tell Susie about her surprise birthday party. Withholding information is lying." No, in this case it isn't. 1 Samuel 16:1–3 offers a clear example of saying less than you know, of giving **a** reason rather than **all** reasons.

To those with under-trained consciences, Satan will say, "Just tell the little white lie. It'll spare feelings and save you a world of grief." He will point to Rahab as a biblically approved example of lying (Josh 2:1–14). He will add 1 Kings 22:17–23 for good measure. In this case, the tempter lives down to the Lord's description of him from John 8:44. He works to help us forget that Scripture is clear and consistent in its condemnation of lying (Rev 21:8, Eph 4:25).

Sometimes the line between saying less than we know and misleading people is a thin one. That line is often defined by motive. Are we intending harm? Are we being self-serving? Are we denying others the opportunity to face reality and make informed decisions? Are we denying others the opportunity to take responsibility for their actions (2 Cor 7:8–12)? Of this we are certain: To cross the line into lying can never be rightly excused. No human motive makes it acceptable to sin. No lie can ever protect the truth.

The myth under discussion claims, "A bit of deception is inevitable, expected, harmless, and maybe even beneficial." How does it present itself to church leaders? Regrettable examples abound. An employee is terminated for misuse of funds, but the reason is never stated. And he's given a glowing letter of recommendation to assist his job search. The stated reasons for the letter? "We wish him no harm." "It's better to avoid conflict." "We didn't want to invite legal action." "Maybe he won't repeat the crime."

A church leader uses an ethnic slur, and an uproar ensues. The temptation is to deny. "It never happened." "You must have misheard." "He wouldn't say such a thing, and if he did, he didn't mean it." We love giving good people every benefit of the doubt. We love taking character and track record into account when evaluating any situation. Is this a recurring problem or one-time rare? (Think of Barnabas in Galatians 2:13.) Does it fit or contradict who we know this person to be? We dare not love denying facts or excusing sin.

A church member inappropriately touches a child. The devil will whisper, "Let's handle this in-house. It's never happened before. We'll be vigilant. It'll never happen again. Think of the scandal if this went public.

Think of the harm to the church." In such situations, there can be no place for denial, deception, or protecting the guilty. The crime must be immediately reported to the authorities. Use the very best discretion in both action and communication AFTER ensuring that the law is followed and all the children are safe.

To offer a far lesser example, people visit church leaders after a Sunday morning sermon. "I don't quite know how to tell you this, but the sermon we heard today wasn't our preacher's. Here's the website from which he got it." It's a crisis of opportunity. If the preacher responds to being caught with "I have sinned. I want to make this right immediately," growth and healing can come. If he responds with denial, excuse, or counter-accusation, Satan has won the day.

Deception destroys. Nowhere is that more true than in the family of God where trust is expected—and essential.

Myth 18

F or the devil and those who follow his lead, hidden agendas are indeed a fact of life. Satan's purported purpose in Genesis 3 was to correct God's false information and to offer Eve an eye-opening new experience. Eve had no clue that "knowing good and evil" meant experiencing sin, pain, shame, death, and separation from God. She never saw the hook that the serpent hid behind a false accusation.

Oppositely, Pilate recognized the hidden agenda of the Jewish leaders who delivered Jesus to him. "For he knew that it was out of envy that they had delivered him up" (Matt 27:18). His wife warned, "Have nothing to do with that righteous man, for I have suffered much because of him today in a dream" (Matt 27:19). Pilate even stated, "I find no guilt in this man" (Luke 23:4). It's one thing to fail to see the hook of a hidden agenda. It's even worse to see it and allow it to destroy.

To his credit, the Roman commander dealing with Paul in Acts 23 learned of the supposedly hidden agenda of those who had vowed to kill the apostle. He acted with haste and wisdom to thwart their plan. When evil agendas become known to good leaders, appropriate action is taken. Good leaders won't let evil hold sway.

Events of Acts 23 remind us of Esther 6. Like Paul's nephew, Mordecai somehow learned of a planned assassination. He exposed the plot to kill the king. Through God's providence, the king was reminded of this good deed at the perfect time to bring the Haman-Mordecai conflict to a head. (See Myth 10).

On a supporting level, Jesus warned of the hidden agendas of false teachers (Matt 7:15–20). Paul echoed that warning (2 Tim 3:1–9). Jude 3–11 re-echoes the same truth.

Of course, most hidden agenda issues don't rise to the level of immediate life and death. But they can be exceedingly destructive. "Don't you think it's about time we started thinking about getting a new preacher?" can be both innocent and wise. Perhaps the current man has indicated a desire to relocate or is planning to retire. However, the statement could be strong evidence of a hidden agenda. "This guy has preached on subjects that hit too close to home. I don't like that" (Gal 4:16, 2 Tim 4:3–4). "This guy just preaches Bible. I want a guy who tells more stories and includes more humor." "This guy expects people to toe the line with doctrine and ethics. We need a man who's more flexible." Thankfully, hidden agendas tend not to stay hidden. The observant soon recognize what's going on. We're blessed to be observant (1 Pet 5:8).

The devil will spin any myth or situation in his effort to harm God's people. If he can't get church leaders to use or tolerate hidden agendas, he will tempt us to invent hidden agendas where none exist. "I don't know why they're asking our family minister to preach more often. Do you think they're trying to force Preacher Joe out of the pulpit?" "I don't know why they changed teachers in the big class. Could it be that they want a teacher who's less loyal to the Book?" And when people who conduct these whisperings get caught, their most common response is "Me? I leveled no accusation. I was only asking a few questions." Yes, questions that betray bad motives and suggest hidden agendas. It's the subject of Proverbs 26:18–19: "Like a madman who throws fire-brands, arrows, and death, is the man who deceives his neighbor and says, 'I was only joking!'" As the next verse makes clear, he knows what fire he's stoking and what pot he's stirring—and neither belongs to the Lord.

Myth 19

PURPOSEFULLY MISHEARING IS A STRONG LEADERSHIP STRATEGY.

P urposeful mishearing is an ancient—and often effective—debate tactic. Add a word to what the speaker said like the devil did in Genesis 3:4. Omit a word or ignore context like the devil did in Matthew 4:5–7. Assume a bad motive and ignore the possibility of a good one (1 Sam 17:28, 2 Sam 10:1–5, Matt 9:1–3 & 9–11). Mishearing includes mis-seeing and mis-thinking. All three practices are fundamentally unfair and dishonest.

Why is this sad strategy so often effective? Most people don't listen carefully. They don't notice the difference of a word here and a phrase there. Confirmation bias is real; we tend to hear what agrees with us and what we expect to hear. Most of us have not been trained to respectfully offer a fair hearing to those who disagree with us. But there's more.

It is both sound and fair to include in our evaluation of a statement consideration of logical conclusions that flow from it. Paul did this powerfully in 1 Corinthians 15.

To paraphrase, "If as you say, the dead are not raised, then Christ is not raised. If Christ is not raised, our gospel is vain, and we are without hope." In no way do we opposes sound thinking. Our intention is to oppose unfair leaps of logic that misrepresent the words of others.

How might this temptation afflict church leaders? From the time of the apostles, "We can't let Gentiles into the church unless they keep Jewish dietary and ceremonial laws. To do so is to insult Moses, the law, and God who gave them both to us." "A Christian cannot eat meat from the public market. It might be from an animal that was sacrificed to an idol. Eating it equals affirming and honoring that idol." But what about current application?

Suppose a good person from a good heart suggests biblically expanding the eldership. What would purposeful mishearing sound like? "How dare you suggest adding elders to our leadership! The men we have now are doing a wonderful job. How dare you call their character into question!" Unless there's far more to the story, this is tragic mishearing. There can be many reasons to suggest adding to an excellent eldership. New elders could be mentored by their more experienced counterparts. Current elders could face unexpected relocation or health crises. Can there be too many qualified shepherds watching for the souls of the flock?

Suppose a good person suggests evaluating the current Bible school program. What might mishearing sound like? "Why would anyone suggest a change to our teaching program? My dear grandparents set it up. It's been working just fine since 1956. If it ain't broke … ."

Gospel content doesn't change. Gospel content cannot be improved. But teaching methods and materials unchanged in more than half a century are unlikely to best serve current learners. "If it ain't broke" has limited application. Fully applied, it allows for no improvement.

Suppose a tech-savvy young man suggests making sermons available worldwide on the web. What would mishearing sound like? "We won't fall victim to modern technology. We won't do PowerPoint. We won't stream our services. If we start streaming, people will stop attending. We won't let men read from their phones during worship. We want people to carry and read their real Bibles. Give the devil an inch and he'll take a mile." Sorry, but we have heard people object to each of these uses of technology among brethren. Technology is a tool that can easily be misused. Misuse by some doesn't forbid faithful use by others. True worship is not about bandwidth, bells, and whistles (John 4:23–24, Ps 100). But asserting that those who advocate increased use of technology are trying to mechanize or dehumanize worship must be rejected as unfair mishearing.

Myth 20

ny leader who presents himself as above being
questioned should strike fear in our hearts. This
attitude is sometimes announced verbally, but
more often it's delivered through actions or by proxy. It
comes in both blunt and thinly veiled forms. Either way,
it's never positive or encouraging.

How do leaders shut down questions? The classic
first move is to pretend not to hear—just to ignore
them. Sometimes leaders offer a dismissive comment:
"How could you ask me that?" or "I won't dignify that
question with a response." Sometimes they employ
humor; they laugh it off. On a stouter level, the motive
of the questioner may be questioned. A false motive may
be assumed and presented as fact. More subtly, some
leaders feign interest, promise answers, but never act. If
worldliness prevails, leaders gossip about the questioner,
effectively discrediting the individual and discouraging
inquiries from others as well.

We so need to watch our motives. As bad as it is to view all questions as rebellions, it's even worse to publicly encourage questions while actually resenting them. In various settings, we have seen good people verbally punished for posing inconvenient questions. We have seen people attacked for making good suggestions. And it breaks our hearts every time it happens. When it happens within the body of Christ, it must break God's heart, too.

There are no mistake-free leaders. There are no sinless leaders (Rom 3:23). Pride crouches at the door to devour any leader who sees himself as above question. Proverbs 16:25, Romans 12:3, and 1 Corinthians 10:12 offer clear warnings.

The devil will use Scripture to foster this myth. When ancient Israel railed on Moses, they actually opposed and insulted God, who appointed Moses. When Israel demanded a king, they were rejecting God's rule far more than Samuel's leadership (1 Sam 8:7). Even when King Saul was at his worst, David refused to raise his hand against God's anointed (1 Sam 24:1–7). David would not allow those under his command to harm Saul (1 Sam 26:1–12). Paul honored this principle in Acts 23:1–5, he teaches us to be careful even about receiving an accusation against a Christian leader (1 Tim 5:19–21). Each of these examples urges caution and respect. None of them suggests that leaders are beyond question or correction.

Why might any godly leader see questions or suggestions as acts of rebellion? Sometimes they are. It's challenging to imagine a rebellion that would not begin with whispers, questions, and other verbal attacks. Moses faced such attacks, on occasion even from his own family (Exod 5:20–21, 14:10–12, 16:2–3; Num 12 & 16). David faced multiple rebellions (1 Sam 29:6, 2 Sam 15–18). Jesus dealt with them as well (Matt 21:23–27, Mark 12:18–27, Luke 20:20–26, John 8:1–12).

Sometimes, church leaders function on a thin edge of fragility. Being hyperaware of their own frailties, they imagine that everyone judges them as harshly as they judge themselves. Thus, every question is a question of qualification, motive, character, and heart. Awareness of this danger should invite us to practice Romans 13:7–8, 1 Timothy 5:17–18, and Hebrews 13:17 to the best of our ability. Church leaders are works in progress—just like the rest of us.

Some church leaders may struggle more deeply with spirituality and godliness than anyone realizes. The issue may not be hyperawareness of frailty, but honest assessment of reality. Others may have been taught zero sum thinking. They may—wrongly and harmfully—think that every discussion is a battle that one side wins and the other side loses. And losing is never an option for those who espouse a zero sum mindset.

Sometimes questions are poorly phrased and suggestions are poorly presented. Brethren can take an accusing tone even when it's counterproductive. They invite defensiveness without realizing that they've done so. They ask private questions in public venues. They put questions before church leaders only after already posing them to everyone else—stunningly out of order!

Sometimes questions are asked in a manipulative or punishing manner. Their purpose lacks nobility. The obvious goal is either to force a desired outcome or to embarrass. "Gotcha" questions are out of order; they don't fit the Golden Rule or the rule of love. We learn much about people when they use such base tactics. Oppositely, we learn even more when an obvious "gotcha" question is available and they graciously choose NOT to ask it.

What can church leaders wisely do with questions that are traps? The wisest course is to study how Jesus handled such questions. Sometimes He refused to answer (Matt 21:27). Sometimes he answered by posing a question of His own (Matt 21:24). Sometimes He answered with a story (Luke 10:21–37). Sometimes He delayed His answer a bit (John 8:6). Sometimes he quoted Scripture and offered a lesson in theology (Mark 12:18–27). To the best of our knowledge, He never deferred or consulted a friend because there was no one wiser than He. But those options are open to us.

Though many of the questions asked to Jesus were wrong and unwise, good questions and suggestions are major blessings. If a question is posed from a good heart, it indicates interest and awareness. It may also indicate a willingness to help. Questions can spur thinking and creativity. Questions can identify growth points and opportunities for improvement. Questions and the dialog that follows can build bonds and strengthen relationships. Questions from a good heart indicate trust. They indicate awareness of approachability: "I'm asking you because you're someone I can talk to." Don't miss the compliment when God offers one.

From a leadership perspective, questions and suggestions aren't nearly as scary as silence. We wish we knew the source of the following frightening adage: "Leaders who do not listen will soon be surrounded by followers who have nothing to say." If our people cease or greatly reduce their input, it's time to learn why—and to effect the needed changes.

Myth 21

WHEN IT COMES TO COMMUNICATION FROM CHURCH LEADERS, CONSISTENCY AND CONGRUENCE ARE OVER-RATED.

As noted already, clarity of communication is strongly promoted in the famous watchman section of Ezekiel 33. Bible students know how Jeremiah's ministry was damaged by the false prophets who offered a pleasant and optimistic message that was the exact opposite of Jeremiah's word from the Lord (Jer 27). Consistency and congruence are major aspects of clarity.

Congruence speaks of actions matching and supporting the spoken message. Think of a child who stammers, "Me not afraid" while cowering with a look of terror in his eyes. Think of an adult yelling, "I AM NOT ANGRY!" through clenched teeth. Wise people know to trust what they see over what they hear. In a church setting, think of an eldership expressing strong support for their preacher while removing him from the pulpit for the next three weeks. Think of an eldership expressing strong unity, but choosing to exclude one or two fellow elders from the next leadership meeting.

Think of a preacher beautifully applying 1 Corinthians 13 to the marriage relationship during his sermon, but yelling rudely at his wife in the parking lot after the morning's service. No one will remember his sermon—at least not positively.

Congruence is about more than how things look, but optics matter. We don't mean to be rude, but even in the church family, people tend to trust actions more than words. And they have biblical backing for this (Acts 1:1 & 10:38, 1 Thess 2:1–12, Prov 20:11). When our example matches our words, communication is empowered and enriched.

Communication consistency includes the intersection of several areas. It's never a blessing for an individual to contradict himself/herself; a pattern of personal self-contradiction always destroys credibility. For church leaders, that loss of credibility also impacts the well-being of the congregation.

Communication consistency also relates to depth and frequency. Is communication depth-appropriate? When we talk, are we speaking meaningfully or merely engaging in chit-chat? Do we flood people with words at times, and then go silent? Regular communication from church leaders shows respect and builds trust. Big communication gaps do the opposite.

Another factor of communication consistency concerns information that is shared by the group (eldership, leadership team, work group) compared to related information that is shared by individual members of the group. If the official message is X but the messages from individuals are Y and Z, communication consistency is shot. The leadership group is in need of help to strengthen its level of communication consistency.

Individual communication styles vary. It would be unfair for hearers to interpret a difference in style as a contradiction in message. Wise leaders look for ways to both be consistent and appear consistent. Wise leaders don't make things more challenging than necessary.

Individual perspectives vary even within excellent, biblically faithful elderships or mission teams. Wise leaders clearly differentiate speaking as individuals from speaking as a representatives of the team. Bluntly, they limit how much they speak as individuals.

Godly church leaders never throw a fellow leader under the bus. It's tragic when a leader says, "I'm sorry the group made this decision. You know I don't agree with them. Don't hold me responsible for this." It's mature and honorable when a leader says, "We prayed, discussed, and did our best to apply biblical principles. The decision we reached is our best effort to honor God and do right."

We love the sweet teaching of 1 Corinthians 1:10; we love unity within God's truth. We respect the reality of Romans 14. Even the best of brethren don't always agree in matters of judgment and application. In such cases we adamantly refuse to "pass judgment on the servant of another," particularly when that "another" is God Himself (Rom 14:4). We neither ignore nor neglect the influence of our behavior on others (Rom 14:7). At the same time, we extend every grace that truth allows us to extend. We assume the best of motives and act to protect one another.

What should we do if one leader does throw another

under the bus? We apply Matthew 5:23–24 and 18:15–17. We apply Acts 18:24–28. As necessary, we apply 1 Timothy 5:19–21. If church leaders don't hold one another accountable, everybody suffers. We hold one another accountable, and we learn from our errors. We do better next time.

Myth 22

TALKING ABOUT A PROBLEM ALWAYS MAKES IT WORSE.

T he most dangerous myths include maximum truth. Certainly, talking about an issue or controversy can make it worse. Jesus's critics effectively employed their knowledge of this truth. They argued against Jesus: "He stirs up the people, teaching throughout all Judea, from Galilee even to this place" (Luke 23:5). Ironically, the chief priests and elders used the very tactic they condemned as they moved the crowd to demand the release of Barabbas and the execution of Jesus (Matt 27:29).

Manipulators artfully switch a few words to radically alter meaning. In the case of "talking about a problem always makes it worse," it's merely replacing *can* with *always*. *Always* asserts certainty while *can* suggests only some degree of hypothetical possibility. It's amazing how often people don't notice the difference, particularly when they're fearful or emotionally invested in an issue. Think of the strong reaction of the king's advisors to Queen Vashti's disobedience (Esth 1:15–17). For them, it threatened the very fabric of society! Oppositely, think about the effective problem-solving discussions of Acts 6:1–7 and 15:1–35.

Paul sets an amazing example of courage in discussing negative events from his life. His transparency in service of the gospel is remarkable. There's the pain and persecution catalog of 2 Corinthians 11:22–29. Struggle and opposition are evident in the joyful letter to Philippi (Phil 1:15–18 and 4:10–20). We see the same level of disclosure in 1 Thessalonians 2:1–2. Most of Paul's inspired letters can accurately be described as problem-solving efforts. Challenges are not swept under the rug.

Scripture offers multiple examples of problems growing worse because they were kept quiet and not addressed in a timely manner. What if Eli had confronted the sins of his sons (1 Sam 2:27–36)? What if David had confronted Amnon's sin against Tamar (2 Sam 13:21)? What if David had confronted Absalom's insolence (2 Sam 15)? Immeasurable pain might have been prevented.

A lesser version of this myth asserts, "If we ignore it (any given problem or conflict), it will go away." This common assertion is anti-history and anti-common sense. It's also unbiblical as implied by Paul's problem-solving letters and by Jesus's letters to the seven churches (Rev 2–3). The basic message of Revelation 2:4–5, 14–16, 20–23; and 3:2–3 & 14–22 remains "clean up what needs to be cleaned up, right what is wrong, or I will—quickly." And that's the Lord's message to His church.

Why is there a tendency among some church leaders to delay, forego, or unwisely extend difficult discussions?

Perhaps at times it's hoping against hope that the Lord will deliver without the need of human action. At times, hesitation flows from extreme fear of conflict, often fueled by painful memories of previous attempts. It can flow from the "paralysis of analysis"—we will act; we just need to ensure that we have fully explored all options before we do. It can flow from ignorance of how much damage is being done. It can flow from laziness. Some discussions are emotionally, physically, intellectually, and spiritually demanding. They devour human resources. Sadly, it can flow from apathy—we just don't have enough love for God's truth or God's people to act. It can flow from lack of faith. We can't see a positive outcome, or we can't see how this can be handled by human effort.

Delaying, foregoing, or unwisely extending difficult discussions can even flow from good motives. "We'd act, but we need to be sure everyone has had his or her say. Until we know that, we must wait." "We'd act, but we have not prayed enough. When we've prayed better, we'll do better." We love prayer, but not when it's misused as a reason to delay obeying God's will.

Myth 23

IF WE'VE TALKED ABOUT A PROBLEM,
WE'VE SOLVED IT.

This myth is the opposite of Myth 22, and it's stunningly common. How many of us have been part of meetings that ended with, "I'm glad that's behind us!" but included no action steps? Such thinking can't accord with Matthew 7:21–23 or James 2. It doesn't fit the parable from Matthew 21:28–32. It won't stand the test of common sense as expressed in the truisms "Talk is cheap," "They tried hard to talk it to death," and "I know what he said he'd do."

From the devil's perspective, Myths 22 and 23 present a "which ditch" situation as mentioned in Myth 8. The devil doesn't care which ditch he baits us into. Either ditch is off the road. He's even happy to let us choose, so long as we deviate from God's way.

Discussion of this myth reminds us of an all-time favorite story. The men of the church discussed lawn care at the church building for more than an hour. Options were explored and rejected. Every suggestion was met with negativity. No possibility seemed fair, desirable, and sustainable. One brother even slipped out of the meeting. As hashing turned to numbing rehashing, they noticed a strange noise. No one could quite make it out. They temporarily adjourned the meeting to investigate. It was the good soul who had slipped out of the meeting. He was on his own mower, clipping the church lawn. Point made—it takes more than talk to get some things done. It's not just a picture that can be worth more than a thousand words.

Examples of over-processing by church leaders abound. There's the preacher search where God provided a clearly superior candidate, but he was no longer available six months later when the deliberations finally ended. There's the proposed building program that never moved forward. By the time discussions led to decisions, the cost of construction had risen to an unfeasible level. There's the exploration of adding a family minister to the church staff. Before consensus was reached, too many young families had relocated into a congregation with a thriving youth ministry. We hope this example is apocryphal: For six weeks, the elders debated who'd be best to visit a beloved but out-of-service member. Regrettably, he died before a decision was made.

Church leaders want to make good and godly decisions. They take their leadership responsibilities most seriously. And Satan is sufficiently ruthless to use those good qualities against them. There's a strong pull to make the perfect decision, but it seldom happens in this sin-damaged world. Perfectionism makes a terrible master. We love the adage, "Make a good decision; then work to make the decision good."

Can we cite biblical examples of those who talked when they should have been acting? Eli said the right words to his evil sons, but he failed to move from words to action (1 Sam 2:22–25 & 3:10–14). James 2:14–17 is even more powerful when read with 1 John 3:18. Mere words won't feed the hungry, clothe the naked, or care for the homeless. The Corinthian Christians were in danger of becoming all talk and no action regarding famine assistance for the brethren in Judea (2 Cor 8:1–9:15). Paul wanted them to know the joy and victory of moving from good words to good deeds.

Can we cite biblical examples of those whose actions exceeded their words, those who over-achieved for the good of others? The Macedonian famine relief effort qualifies (1 Cor 8). Stephanas, his family, and at least two of their friends qualify (1 Cor 16:15–19). Both Timothy and Epaphroditus qualify (Phil 2:10–30). Paul was confident that Philemon would over-deliver as well (Phlm 20–21).

Merely talking about a problem seldom solves it. It's not even the best place to begin the process—we'd reserve first place for prayer. There are occasions when no solution exists and our goal must be achieving acceptance, choosing to be content with God's reality (2 Cor 12:7–10). When solutions or improvements are possible, we're blessed to move from discussion to action. Wise leaders help establish appropriate action steps, goals, and timelines. And they model effective communication as they do so.

Myth 24

MANSPLAINING IS WHAT MEN DO.

W e respect the fact that Scripture speaks of godly men serving as elders and filling other formal leadership roles in the church (1 Tim 2:8–15 & 3:1–13, Titus 1). At the same time, we strongly affirm that men and women are equally made in the image of God (Gen 1:26–27). We know that godly women are pillars of work and spirituality in many healthy congregations. We know the Bible presents many examples of heroic and exemplary women—think of Deborah, Jael, Hannah, Esther, Ruth, Elizabeth, Mary, Anna, Priscilla, Phoebe, and Lydia. We know women were exceedingly important in the earthly ministry of Jesus (Luke 8:1–3). We know there is no difference in worth or status between men and women in the kingdom of God (Gal 3:26–29). And we know that culture and tradition affect how men treat women and women treat men.

Mansplaining is a fairly recent word. Googling the definition leads to some version of "the explanation of something by a man, typically to a woman, in a manner regarded as condescending or patronizing." In its rawest form it's "Don't worry your pretty little head about this. Such things are better left to men" or "Women are not the church's decision makers. Why we do what we do is none of their business." We hope you recognize this as patently insulting on numerous levels. More subtly it's "Let's not bother the ladies with this information. We have things well in hand." More cynically it's "If we start explaining some of our decisions, they'll expect us to explain every decision." More traditionally it's "We've always done it this way. If it ain't broke ... ."

To paint with the broadest of brushes, in many cultures ladies process, make decisions, and implement decisions more relationally than men. They use more words, they listen with more heart, and they give more consideration to the feelings of others. Men tend to live on the task-orientation, "git 'er done," side of life. Each approach has costs and advantages depending on the nature of the task and the nature of the organization. In the church—a family of redeemed sacrificial volunteers guided by love—there's much to commend a strongly relational approach. You might revisit the discussion of Myth 4.

To address a possible elephant in the room, we're not addressing mansplaining in political or even sociological terms. Our concern is limited to how Satan would use natural differences to create ungodly divisions. We don't want to hand the devil a crowbar with which to pry us apart. We don't want to widen any crevice that the devil could exploit. We want to encourage wise application of

Matthew 10:16, "Be wise as serpents and innocent as doves."

Christian ladies live under notable pressure. Their secular counterparts accuse them of being doormats and sellouts. "You perpetuate demeaning archaic stereotypes by submitting to your husbands" (Eph 5:22–33). "You allow men to lead in areas where you know you are capable" (1 Tim 3, Titus 1). "You do the bulk of the day-to-day work, you give generously, you make up the majority of the church, and then you let men talk to you like you don't have a brain."

Insult and condescension have no place within the kingdom of God. All Christians are mandated to "Pay to all what is owed them . . . respect to whom respect is owed, honor to whom honor is owed" (Rom 13:7). We dare not let the world around us shape our minds, dictate our behavior, or control our communication (Rom 12:1–2). We dare not discourage strong, spiritual fellow-servants who do so much to bless God's kingdom.

Myth 25

ANY REASON IS AS GOOD AS THE REASON.

In our discussion of Myth 14, we documented that leaders are not obligated to tell everything that they know (1 Sam 16:1–3). What we say must be true, but complete disclosure is not biblically mandated. At the same time, within wise limits, transparency is a virtue. People fear secrecy. They love to be kept informed.

Myth 25 is specific. It speaks of offering a reason—a lesser or insufficient reason—for a choice or action when THE reason could legitimately and beneficially be stated. Why would Christian leaders ever do so? A sad and blunt answer: because they can. "We're in control. It's in our power to disclose only what we want to disclose." While factually correct, such thinking is dangerous. It invites pride and division. It smacks of "in group / out group" thinking. It invites an us-versus-them mentality.

A second reason some leaders don't share core reasons: "We need to train our people to trust us. If we always explain ourselves, they'll always expect an explanation. We need to teach them about faith." We assert that there will be plenty of situations where full explanations can't be offered—we don't need to create additional opportunities. We further assert that this is not the best way to build trust. Treat people like family whenever possible. Let them in on the process. Let your example of wise, prayerful, and biblically-guided decision making serve as a pattern for others.

Some share a lesser reason even when THE reason could be stated because THE reason is less than noble. Examples of less-than-noble reasons include because we wanted to, because it was easier, because we've always done it that way, and because we didn't have the energy to explore other options.

"Any reason is as good as THE reason" often indicates belief in another myth—either no one will notice or no one will care. Not noticing couldn't be desirable. It speaks of distraction or disengagement. Not caring would be even worse. It speaks of apathy or abandonment. None of this speaks of a vibrant God-honoring body of believers.

But there's more. "Either no one will notice or no one will care" is patently false. The bright, awake, and dedicated will both notice and care. It's like Revelation 3:4; even within a severely struggling group, there are often "a few names . . . who have not soiled their garments." To cite the Old Testament concept, there will be a faithful remnant in whom faith lives and through whom God works. And we dare not discourage their good hearts!

What's the harm in sharing a reason when THE

reason could be shared? For people who think well, it's insulting. They may not say much, but they're likely to think, "You expect us to believe that? It doesn't make sense. What's being hidden, and why are you hiding it? I wonder what else you're not telling us? Do they really think they're that much smarter than the rest of us?" Withholding information without adequate reason seems unfair. It feels wrong. It tempts people to question both motive and character. But those are just the obvious negative results.

Christian living is far more than NOT sinning. Christian living and leadership include proactive stewardship and creative service. In every circumstance we ask, "How can I use this to bring glory to God? How can this opportunity be seized to broaden the kingdom? How can my words and actions in this moment honor Christ and adorn the gospel?

Through forthcoming, transparent, and helpful explanations, church leaders help others see their good hearts. They promote healthy openness and truth telling. They model good practices for developing church leaders. They show good faith and build trust.

Myth 26

BECAUSE WE SAID SO.

W e strongly disagree with the famous line from an ancient John Wayne movie, "Never apologize, mister; it's a sign of weakness" (*She Wore a Yellow Ribbon*, 1949). We just as strongly disagree with the assertion that "because we said so" is a wise or helpful explanation from church leaders. Though it sometimes has a place in parenting—admittedly there's not always time or energy to explain—it's not a primary tool even in a home with young children.

We'd never assert that every decision must be explained in detail. Leaders are often privy to information that they cannot share with others. When that's the case, our strong recommendation is to say, "I'm sorry, but we have information that we're not free to share. Please know that we're doing our best in light of all that we know." In our judgment, that's fair, honest, and forthcoming.

"Because we said so" doesn't come across well. Many view that statement as an assertion of raw power. Some hear it as "Our judgment is above question"—see Myth 20. Some hear it as "We could explain, but we don't want to." Others hear it as "This matter is above your pay-grade. You don't have the standing to merit an explanation." Those with fragile egos can hear it as "We'd offer an explanation, but you wouldn't have the capacity to understand it." There are just too many ways these words can go wrong. They may also be examples of "mansplaining." See Myth 24.

Offering "because we said so" as an explanation runs against the grain of Scripture. It doesn't follow God's example. Though God never owes anyone an explanation for His actions, He frequently—and graciously—reveals His heart. We mentioned earlier how God revealed His plans regarding Sodom and Gomorrah to His friend Abraham (Gen 18:17–21). God explained to David why he would not be allowed to build the temple (2 Sam 7). Time and again God explained to His people why He was angry with them and was punishing them (Isa 1, Jer 2, Ezek 2, Amos 1). When Daniel prayed about his struggles to understand God's prophecy of a seventy-year captivity followed by release, God sent an angel to explain (Dan 9).

During His earthly ministry, Jesus frequently offered explanations to His disciples and others. He explained why His disciples fasted less than John's followers (Matt 9:14–17). He explained why His disciples did not keep the Pharisees' version of the Sabbath restrictions (Matt 12:1–8). He explained why He so frequently taught through parables (Matt 13:10–17). He explained why His disciples failed to cast out a demon (Matt 17:17–21). In Mark 2:1–12 He explained why He used "Son, your sins are forgiven" to heal a paralytic man, and His explanation blesses us to this day.

Paul explained his delay in visiting the Christians in Rome (Rom 1:8–13). He explained why the church in Rome should assist Phoebe (Rom 16:1–2). He explained why Stephanas and his household should be respected and imitated (1 Cor 16:15–18).

The conclusion is clear; the Bible strongly supports keeping people in the loop rather than in the dark. While it provides many positive examples, Scripture offers no example of wise leaders asserting, "You'll just have to trust us," or "Either you trust us or you don't." We appreciate this demonstration of psychological insight. It runs counter to human nature to accept a demand for trust. We know the axiom: Trust must be earned. Good people will extend a degree of trust to new or unknown leaders, but they do so watchfully. They won't keep trusting without reason. Trustworthiness must be demonstrated, and wise leaders seize every opportunity to earn the respect of those whom they serve.

Myth 27

I t's a classic suggestion in test-taking workshops. True / false items that present absolutes are generally false. There are exceptions, but when you must guess, wisdom says to choose false. And we know why. Speaking broadly, this world is diverse and unpredictable. Humans are even worse. There's virtually nothing that everybody knows. Even some things that we used to know currently escape us.

From the perspective of church leaders, the "everybody knows" myth is sometimes more accurately "everybody who wants to know already knows." "We've told them in the assembly. We put it in print. We posted it across platforms. There's no way to have missed it." No insult intended, but humans have amazing ability to miss important messages.

Sometimes "everybody knows" is more accurately "we're tired of telling this. We've extended amazing effort. Nobody could rightly expect more from us." When those thoughts come, our recommendation is

"Look for your second wind. People might be at the point of beginning to hear."

"Everybody knows" can be an affirmation of common knowledge. "Everybody knows the sun rises in the east. Everybody knows water is wet. Everybody knows elders rule, feed, lead, protect, and shepherd the church." But people who don't recognize figures of speech want to explain rotation and revolution to give a scientifically accurate description of daylight and dark. Engineers will ask, "What do you mean by wet? Wet compared to what?" Those of us with farm backgrounds will remember adding a surfactant to the spray tank to "make the water wetter." And not everyone knows 1 Timothy 3, Titus 1, and 1 Peter 5.

Knowing human nature, the Bible is HUGE on repetition and reminder. Genesis 22 offers a stunning example. We know that Isaac is Abraham's son, the son of his old age, the son of God's promise. Yet the text repeats "son" like a drumbeat. It even includes "father." Within the psalms there are stunningly similar sections. Within Proverbs the value of wisdom is echoed again and again.

The New Testament gives us four gospel accounts. Among Paul's letters some scholars describe Galatians as a "mini-Romans" and note the similarity between major sections of Ephesians and Colossians. Jude and 2 Peter plow much of the same ground. Peter overtly states, "Therefore I intend always to remind you of these qualities, though you know them and are established in the truth that you have. I think it right as long as I am in the body, to stir you up by way of reminder" (2 Pet 1:12–13). And the Hebrew writer reminds us that even important truth can slip from us—and we can slip from it (Heb 2:1–4 & 5:12).

There's virtually nothing that everybody knows, but the danger of this myth is manifold. For anything communicated during an assembly, some members will be absent. Others will be present in body, but not fully engaged. Some will be in a world of their own and won't hear in context.

What do we suggest? Go multimodal. For important information, communicate orally and visually across platforms. Use different speakers with their different styles, talents, and points of connection.

Apply Galatians 6:9 to church communication. Refuse to "grow weary of doing good." Realize the virtue and value of persistence. Believe God's promise and rely on it for motivation: "in due season we will reap if we do not give up."

When it comes to communication, groups travel more slowly than individuals. The rule of thumb within the communication literature can be summarized: "When you get really tired of communicating, you've probably made a good start." We must love God's people enough to go the second, third, and fourth miles.

Myth 28

CONFLICT: WE HAVE TO SHUT THIS
DOWN.

This discussion parallels and extends the content of Myths 9, 14, and 22. Conflict terrifies many church leaders. They see any kind or level of conflict as opposing Psalm 133, Ephesians 4:1–6, and the precious unity prayer of Jesus in John 17. They see any kind of conflict as an abomination to God, as sowing "discord among brothers" (Prov 6:19). It will bless us to take a broader view.

As strongly as we value unity and pursue peace, conflict isn't always totally bad. The debate that led to the Jerusalem Conference of Acts 15 was stout and dangerous. But the meeting described in Acts 15 was blessed and strengthening. Truth prevailed. Grace prevailed. The church was more focused and united after the meeting than before.

The interpersonal conflict described in Acts 15:36–41 teaches in an amazing manner. Barnabas and Paul had incompatible judgments about John Mark. Counter to the thinking of many, the text offers no clue as to who was right or which opinion was better. It's possible neither leader was in error—that each made valid judgments from his individual perspective. The text discloses the resolution of the matter. Rather than one mission team, two moved forward with the gospel. This much is clear: Conflict sometimes ends with good change. We're impressed that the Bible offers no record of Paul or Barnabas seeking to justify his judgment or in any way speaking evil of the other person.

There are several good reasons to be careful about trying to shut down verbal disagreement. First, it's stunningly difficult to do. Telling people NOT to discuss a matter tends to backfire. As Mark 1:40–45 documents, even the Lord could not secure cooperation in limiting communication.

People inherently resent being told not to talk about a subject or issue. The devil is skilled at misusing efforts to limit or stop discussion. While godly leaders know their intentions are honorable—"We need time to cool down. We need to pray and think. Right now the rhetoric is generating far more heat than light"—that's not what the devil helps people hear. He aims for "There they go again, being hyper-controlling. Truth has nothing to fear from discussion. They're hiding something. They can't tell us what to do. What don't they want us to know?"

Caution is wise because conflict includes an energizing element of discomfort. That discomfort can move people to action—action that isn't always bad. We do not want to interrupt any process that leads to godly action. That's exactly what Acts 6:1–7 describes. Conflict arose, leaders faced it honestly, a solution was proposed, the entire group was invited to help implement the solution, the godly leaders never stopped leading, and the whole church was blessed.

It's wise to be cautious in how we attempt to limit communication—even negative words—because people often apply the counsel of their leaders in unwise and unintended ways. Leaders can prayerfully and carefully suggest, "Please tone down your words. Please be extra respectful. For the good of everyone, weigh your words before you speak. Please choose to say far less than you think." What some hear is, "If you're telling us not to talk, we'll give you what you think you want. If you want silence, we'll give you SILENCE." If we're not both careful and blessed, we'll shut down far more than we intended.

Except in the rarest of circumstances, we strongly recommend trying to influence the nature and quality of the communication rather than trying to stop it (Titus 1:10–11). Pray for everyone. Stay civil. Be gracious. Listen and learn. Give everyone the benefit of every doubt. Keep trusting God to do more and better than we can.

Myth 29

WORK HARD ENOUGH AND YOU CAN EXTINGUISH COMMUNICATION ERRORS.

We love giving our best to God (Matt 22:36–38, Rom 12:1–2, Col 3:23–24). We love giving God credit and honor for everything that's good (Jas 1:17). We love knowing that God has amazing ability to change lives. That's what makes this myth so dangerous. To state it in its most religious form, "Work and pray hard enough, and God will help you extinguish all communication errors." It sounds great—biblical and faithful, but it's just not true.

On every level, we love to tell our Bible students, "Always trust the text. The Bible is God's word. It is our standard." Trusting the text includes trusting James 3. Save the Lord Himself, everyone we know or have known has at times stumbled "in what he says" (Jas 3:2). We don't offer this as excuse or reason, just as a statement of fact.

We know Satan twists James 3 as he does the rest of Scripture. "Since the tongue is an untamable, unruly evil, why try? Why beat your head against a wall? Why not spend your efforts on doable tasks?" If that doesn't work, he offers, "God is so good. He understands human communication struggles. He takes weakness into account (Ps 103:11–14). Since God cuts humanity so much slack, why don't you cut yourself a little slack, too? What sense does it make to hold yourself to an impossible standard?" Of course, Ephesians 4:11–16 and 1 Peter 1:13–16 falsify Satan's errant teaching. James 3 is an appeal to caution, insight, and purposeful effort to keep our speech both godly and consistent.

The fact that everyone, at one time or another, sins with the tongue doesn't discount Ephesians 4:29–32 or Colossians 4:5–6. We keep choosing wisdom and gracious speech. We battle corrupting talk and embrace godly speech that builds people up. To use the academic language, we embrace continual quality improvement.

What, then, are the dangers of "work hard enough and you can extinguish communication errors"? As phrased, the emphasis is on human effort and accomplishment. James 3 moves from discussing the tongue to differentiating worldly and godly wisdom. Without God's gracious help, our improvements will be marginal at best.

As phrased, "extinguish communication errors" sets perfection as the standard of success. It gives Satan place to claim, "Unless you have achieved perfection, you have utterly failed. Unless you have achieved perfection, there is no hope." Our perfect God and Savior is our standard (Matt 5:48, Eph 4:15). Every step we take toward Their blessed examples is a spiritual victory. We never stop moving toward Them, and we never falsely claim to have arrived (Phil 3:12–16). We continually acknowledge and appreciate Their help (1 John 2:1–2). We find joy in knowing that Jesus draws us toward Himself. That joy doubles as we remember God draws near to us as we draw near to Him (Jas 4:8).

In addition to the teaching of James 3 and our common experience, there's another way we know that we'll never eliminate all communication errors. The bulk of communication includes other people. Even if, as church leaders, your next communication effort were flawless—the right words in the right tone at the right time from the right heart fully supported by Scripture—it would not be heard flawlessly. Even the best people just aren't that good.

While we cannot eliminate every communication error, we're blessed to try. Trying is a powerful way to draw nearer to God. Trying makes us more trusting in His word and more reliant on His power (and we'll pray better). Trying feeds humility and opposes pride. Trying builds unity with fellow disciples. Trying enhances our patience with and support for fellow strugglers.

Myth 30

ONE PERSON CAN'T MAKE MUCH DIFFERENCE IN CHURCH COMMUNICATION.

W e have spoken of God's church as a kingdom of right relationships. Throughout this brief book, we have used a plural tone and focused on communication between people. It may seem odd to conclude by discussing the influence of a single godly person.

Scripture powerfully documents the power of one person who stands with God. When the whole world was so evil that "the Lord regretted that he had made man," one righteous person changed everything (Gen 6:6). When "Noah found favor in the eyes of the Lord," God used him and his family to save humanity.

Through one man, God started the nation through whom the Christ would come (Gen 12:1–4). When God wanted to deliver His people from seven years of fierce famine, one man played the central human role (Gen 37–50). Though God graciously gave him a spokesman, one man was called to lead the Exodus (Exod 3–4). The judges of ancient Israel often recruited help, but God raised them up one at a time. One prophet addressed David's sin with Bathsheba and moved the king to repentance (2 Sam 12). One faithful man stood against hundreds of false prophets on Mount Carmel (1 Kgs 18). As a single voice of truth, Jonah—though exceedingly resistant—moved ancient Nineveh to repentance. Jeremiah stood in Jerusalem as a singular faithful voice against many false prophets. After a gap of 430 years, God raised just one voice to preach repentance and prepare the way of the Lord (Matt 3). God providentially used one voice, a Pharisee, to save Peter and John from death (Acts 5:33–40). He used another single voice to save Paul later (Acts 23:11–30).

How Satan must hate such singular faithful voices! They thwarted major plots, saving both lives and souls. Worse, they remind us of what God can do when even one person lives and speaks faithfully for Him.

This is a book for church leaders. *Leaders* is, by definition, plural. The church is richly blessed when leaders stand together as one to serve, lead, and protect. Practically speaking, standing together as one often begins with each one choosing to stand faithfully with God.

It's always right to stand faithfully with God. We will one day stand individually before the judgment seat of Christ (2 Cor 5:10). Individual responsibility rests with each of us (Gal 6:4–5). When we stand for what we know to be right, we never know who will be emboldened to stand with us. Would Barak be listed in Hebrews 11:32 if Deborah had not called him out of his fear (Judg 4:6–8)? Would Saul have become the apostle Paul without the help of Barnabas (Acts 9:26–28, 11:25–26)? Clearly, God used the courage of Deborah and Barnabas to bring out the best in others.

We dare not claim that one person who speaks faithfully for the Lord always prevails against evil and unbelief. Jeremiah could not change the fate of his nation. Centuries before, even two faithful voices—Joshua and Caleb—could not move their people to choose faith. Despite His perfection, Jesus was executed as a blasphemer.

Why embrace an ethic of clear, courageous, righteous, and loving communication when there's no guarantee of immediate positive result? Why hold ourselves to God's standard when many don't understand why we do? The first great reason is that God is always God, and right is always right. A second major reason flows from Esther 4:14, "And who knows whether you have not come to the kingdom for such a time as this?" We don't know what the Lord will do next or whether He will allow us a role in His plan.

We sometimes describe our answer to the "why try even if you stand alone" question as "passing the mirror test." On one level, we hold up the mirror of God's word and hold ourselves accountable to it. Since God does, we should. On another level, at the end of each day we want to be able to look ourselves in the mirror and say, "I tried to be faithful today. I tried to say what needed to be said and to do what needed to be done. With my life and my words, I said to all, 'I am on the Lord's side.'" Any day we do that is a good day—a blessed day that leads to an even better tomorrow (Matt 25:20–21).

SCRIPTURE INDEX

About the Authors

Bill Bagents earned his master's degree in counselor education from Auburn University and doctor of ministry from Amridge University. He is currently professor of ministry, counseling, and biblical studies with Heritage Christian University. He has served as an elder, deacon, and minister. Bill has worked as a counselor with the Alpha Center in Florence; he has also taught counseling courses in Bangladesh, Nigeria, the Philippines, and South Africa.

Laura Lynn Stegall Bagents is a career classroom teacher with Florence City Schools. She earned degrees from Auburn University, the University of North Alabama, and the University of Alabama (EdD 2008). Her church-related teaching has included children's Bible classes in local congregations as well as adjunct roles with Heritage Christian University and classes for ladies and children in Albania and on the Western Cape of South Africa.

Also by Heritage Christian University Press in cooperation with Heritage Christian Leadership Institute

Lead Like the Lord: Leadership Lessons from Jesus
by W. Kirk Brothers (2021)

Counseling for Church Leaders: A Practical Guide
by Bill Bagents and Rosemary Snodgrass (2021)

HERITAGE
CHRISTIAN UNIVERSITY
PRESS

CYPRESS
PUBLICATIONS
An Imprint of Heritage Christian University Press

To see full catalog of Heritage Christian University Press
and its imprint Cypress Publications, visit
www.hcu.edu/publications

www.ingramcontent.com/pod-product-compliance
Lightning Source LLC
Chambersburg PA
CBHW050733030426
42336CB00012B/1550